geoff thompson

fear

FEAR – THE FRIEND OF EXCEPTIONAL PEOPLE

Geoff Thompson

First edition published in 1995
Reprinted 1995, 1996 (twice), 1997, 1998, 1999, 2001, 2013

Geoff Thompson Ltd.
PO Box 307
Coventry
CV3 9YP
United Kingdom

www.geoffthompson.com

Printed and bound in Great Britain by 4edge Limited.

ISBN 13: 978 0 95692 155 0

geoff thompson

fear

the friend of exceptional people

About the Author

Geoff Thompson is a BAFTA winning Writer.

He has written forty books (published in 21 languages), he is a multi-award-winning screenwriter, an acclaimed playwright (he was invited into the prestigious Royal Court Young Writers Group) and author of hundreds of articles, many published in national magazines and broadsheets, including The Times.

He is also one of the most senior martial arts in the world today, holding the rank of Hanshi (8th dan).

Geoff's autobiography, Watch My Back, was adapted into a major motion picture, (Clubbed). It premiered in London's West End, Birmingham and Paris and was nominated for a BIFFA award. He has also adapted his first novel, Red Mist (Last Will), into a feature film for cinema.

Geoff's third feature film for cinematic release, (Romans) has been optioned by The Tea Shop & Film Company in London. His play Fragile premiered to five star reviews at the Belgrade Theatre in 2012.

Geoff has recently enjoyed the Number 1 slot on iTunes with his inspirational podcasts.

Geoff lives between Coventry West Midlands and Islington London.

www.geoffthompson.com

Other books and DVDs by Geoff Thompson:

Books:

Red Mist
Watch My Back: The Geoff Thompson Autobiography
The Elephant and the Twig: The Art of Positive Thinking
The Great Escape: The 10 Secrets to Loving Your Life and Living Your Dreams
Shape Shifter: Transform Your Life in 1 Day
Stress Buster: How to Stop Stress From Killing You
The Formula: The Secret to a Better Life
Real Grappling
Real Punching
Real Kicking
Real Head, Knees and Elbows
Dead or Alive: The Choice is Yours
Three Second Fighter: The Sniper Option
Weight Training: For the Martial Artist
The Pavement Arena: Adapting Combat Martial Arts to the Street
Animal Day: Pressure Testing the Martial Arts
The Fence: The Art of Protection
The Art of Fighting Without Fighting
The Throws and Takedowns of Judo
The Throws and Takedowns of Sombo Russian Wrestling
The Throws and Takedowns of Freestyle Wrestling
The Throws and Takedowns of Greco-Roman Wrestling

The Ground Fighting Series
Pins: The Bedrock
The Escapes
Chokes and Strangles
Arm Bars and Joint Locks
Fighting From Your Back
Fighting From Your Knees

DVDs:

Animal Day: Pressure Testing the Martial Arts
Animal Day Part Two: The Fights
Three Second Fighter: The Sniper Option
Throws and Takedowns Vols. 1–6
Real Punching Vols. 1–3
The Fence

Ground Fighting Series
Vol 1 Pins: The Bedrock
Vol 2 The Escapes
Vol 3 Chokes and Strangles
Vol 4 Arm Bars and Joint Locks
Vol 5 Fighting From Your Back
Vol 6 Fighting From Your Knees

Advanced Ground Fighting Vols. 1–3
Pavement Arena Part 1
Pavement Arena Part 2: The Protection Pyramid
Pavement Arena Part 3: Grappling – The Last Resort
Pavement Arena Part 4: Fit To Fight

For more details visit www.geoffthompson.com

Thank you very much to Rachael Osborne for doing
a fabulous job on editing this book and keeping
me in grammatical shape.

I would like to dedicate this book to my beautiful daughter
Jennie because I love her with all my heart,
and to my most beautiful lady Sharon,
with all my love and big kisses.

Contents

Introduction

'We are generally afraid to become that which we can glimpse in our most perfect moments; under the most perfect conditions, under conditions of greatest courage, we enjoy and even thrill to the god-like possibilities we see in ourselves at such peak moments, and yet simultaneously shiver with weakness, awe and fear before the same possibilities.'

Abraham Maslow

Working one's way through a life that is fraught with intangible confrontation, in an adrenal-loaded body that was designed for conflicts of a physical nature (fight or flight), it is a small wonder that most people go to their graves with their best songs still in them. Evidently the adrenal syndrome is better suited to mortal conflict (fighting or escaping the sabre-toothed tiger) and is left wanting in a time when confrontation may be a boardroom meeting, high mortgage rates or a row with your partner.

Tangible confrontation on a base level – where the adrenal rush adds speed, power and anaesthesia to response – has been succeeded by confrontations of a rather vague nature; a run in with the boss, perhaps a business decision, even traffic jams are enough to trigger our rather sensitive adrenals into action. In these situations adrenalin is released but not utilised because neither fight nor flight is necessary. It would be unreasonable and antisocial (though often tempting) to strike a vindictive boss and unwise (though very common) to run away from confrontations in the home. So, very often, we find ourselves infused with adrenalin that can find no physical (or behavioural) release from our bodies.

This creates an inner pressure (and an eventual explosion – like the cork of a shaken champagne bottle) that can have a devastating and life-changing effect. When the explosion does finally occur it is usually without warning or provocation.

Concurrently the reasoning process, misreading the feeling of adrenalin for fear, builds a subconscious periphery that imprisons the part of us that wants to achieve. Fear is what keeps people ordinary.

It is said that knowledge dispels fear. Have a good look around you and have a good look at yourself. How many people do you know who are truly happy with their lot? Society is full of underachievers: not because we lack potential or courage, but because we lack an understanding of our own bodily reactions to confrontation. Adrenalin often catalyses panic, causing plans to be aborted or changed for fear of the consequences, or fear of fear itself.

Twenty-five centuries ago General Sun Tzu said, 'If you know your enemy and know yourself, you need not fear the outcome of a hundred battles.' Knowing yourself is understanding that fear is both a friend and an enemy. It's OK to be scared, we all feel fear, all of us. And we need it to keep our species alive. In this sense fear is a friend, it can be controlled and it can be employed as a life-changing fuel. It is only when we panic that fear becomes the mind killer.

Ian Botham succinctly advised us that 'life is not a rehearsal'. We have one chance to do something great, something worthwhile, something life-changing – and this is it. Most people are living lives that they don't want to live. Why? Because they are imprisoned in safe bet comfort zones that they dare not exit for fear of failure, success, change, risk, ridicule or whatever. They dream of better jobs, happier relationships, nicer cars, success and fulfilment but those ideals are seldom realised because lying ominously between fancy and fact is FEAR.

The blame for failure is frequently off-loaded with the *excuse syndrome*. 'If it wasn't for… I could really do something with my life.'

Most of us sit in the driveway of life watching it go by, too scared to pull out into the traffic, frightened to use fuel, and afraid in case we crash. Many have the dynamite needed to explode into an adventurous life but lack the courage and understanding to light the fuse.

What most fail to realise is that whether you are facing a big business deal, a showdown with the boss or a couple of muggers up an alleyway you will feel fear. It is as much its unexpectedness as the feeling itself that turns men to mice.

When life presents us with a confrontation of any kind we will feel fear and its manifestation carries many disguises with varying degrees of intensity. It will always be present.

The purpose of this book is to help break down the prison walls by educating people in the mechanics of fear. How to recognise, understand and subsequently control fear and employ it as an ally.

This is not a book about phobias, though the symptoms and remedies herein are paralleled with those of the phobic condition. When dealing with fear at most levels the response of exposure therapy is the same. One systematically confronts a fear until desensitisation occurs.

Fear never goes away!

I learned very early on in my practice that whilst we can lose a fear of a certain thing or situation we will never get rid of fear completely, it will always be there whilst we continue to expand. Rather we learn to recognise and control fear, deeming it a powerful tool that will aid us in our response to confrontation.

The intent of this book is to allow people to see themselves from the inside out so that panic is replaced by understanding, and discomfort by relief.

The world is your oyster; it is only you holding yourself back.

Chapter One

What is Fear?

'The coward and the hero both feel the same feelings [of fear], the only difference between the two is that the hero handles the feelings and the coward does not.'

Cus Damatio (trainer to Mike Tyson)

What is fear? How can one define it? The English dictionary informs us that fear is 'an unpleasant, often strong emotion caused by anticipation or awareness of danger.'

In layman's terms, when the brain senses danger it triggers adrenalin, a human turbocharge brought on by awareness and anticipation to aid fight or flight. This unpleasant strong emotion often causes terror immobilisation, or the freeze syndrome, in the recipient. Adrenalin is a little like fuel injection or turbodrive in a sports car and action is the metaphoric accelerator.

By engaging the clutch in a car and pressing the accelerator you utilise the turbo and the car moves at a faster speed. However, if you sit at the traffic lights pressing your foot on the accelerator without engaging the clutch, there will be no movement and fuel will be wasted.

Similarly, by engaging action (fight or flight) when we feel fear, we utilise the turbodrive of adrenalin, and trigger a fast and speedy spontaneous response. However, if action is not engaged and panic sets in, the excess energy will overwhelm us.

Positive Body Accelerator

Your positive body accelerator is action. When you act (engage the clutch), by confronting your fear, adrenalin is utilised positively, adding vigour to your response.

Negative Body Accelerator

Your negative body accelerator is panic, caused when the reasoning process mistakes adrenalin for fear. Excess adrenalin is triggered by panic (but not utilised) and the body is flooded, leaving the recipient overwhelmed and often frozen in the face of ensuing danger.

If you find yourself in a confrontational situation and do not or cannot act, increasing panic will trigger more adrenalin. Like the car, you will be pressing the accelerator without engaging the clutch.

In the gap between confrontation and action adrenalin can be controlled with diaphragmatic breathing (deep controlled breathing through the nose). This triggers what is known as the parasympathetic nervous system, which slows the release of adrenalin. Also, the knowledge that it is OK to be scared and that fear is a natural occurrence can offer great solace when the butterflies are invading your intestinal tract and your kneecaps are doing an involuntary bossanova.

In primeval days when mankind had to fight to live and eat, the feeling of fear was an everyday occurrence that would have felt as natural and as common as eating or drinking. In today's society, where confrontation is less tangible, the act of fighting or running for our lives is no longer a part of everyday living. So when a situation arises that causes the adrenalin to flow, we neither welcome, use or like it because, unlike our prehistoric ancestors, we are unfamiliar with it. We panic. Psychologists call it the fight or flight syndrome.

In moments of danger or confrontation the body releases chemicals from the adrenal gland that hit and go through the bloodstream like a speeding train, preparing the body for fight or flight, deeming it stronger, faster and partially, sometimes completely, anaesthetised to pain. The more demanding the situation, the bigger the build-up and adrenalin release: the bigger the release, the better the performance (running or fighting). However, by the same count, the bigger the build-up and release, the harder it is to control.

Subsequently, because the adrenalin often lies unutilised in the body, it builds up like a pressure cooker and explodes into other aspects of our lives. This could be in the car as road-rage, or in the home by shouting at your partner or children.

If the adrenalin is not pushed outward it often turns inward and becomes anxiety, a constant background shadow that can creep quite easily into depression. We become afraid of the feeling of fear, and the very act of feeling afraid triggers more adrenalin and more fear. You end up on a downward spiral of fear and adrenalin. This exhausts the mind and confusion and depression can be the result.

The worst part of this cycle is normally the very first time that fear is felt about something. People tend to allow that first encounter to overwhelm them and then live in dread of it happening again. Of course this dread becomes a fear in its own right and we often end up more frightened of the feelings associated with fear than the actual object of our fear.

... it is imperative to remind yourself from ... that the feelings cannot hurt you on their own ... that, whilst uncomfortable, they should be accepted and not fought. Acceptance is the first step. It is hard for your mind to blackmail you with threats of fear if you tell yourself, and continue to tell yourself, that you accept the feelings and that as long as they continue to come, you will continue to accept them. Acceptance is the way to stop the fear-adrenalin-fear cycle. Accept the feelings. Let them go through you like a wave. Examine them, even ask for more. I know that this might sound absurd but it is the way to combat anxiety attacks.

What I try to do is allow the feelings to go through me like a wave and then I try and make them bigger, I ask for more. And guess what? The moment you accept and ask for more, the moment you fully accept that you can live with it, is the very moment that it starts to go away. Your trepidation and the thought of feeling fear actually triggers fear. So by accepting, even asking for more, you take away that trepidation and so stop the fear in the very early stages.

Challenge it when it starts. Come on then, come in, let's feel you. More please. This will bring respite. If your mind is tired it will take a bit of time to get it strong again; just like an injury or any illness there is a recovery time and you may get setbacks, the feelings may start again, but you must stop them at every juncture. Every time you feel fear you must muster up the courage to go through the whole process again until, in the end, it stops trying. And it will; it just takes time. The sooner you start accepting, the sooner the healing begins.

Adrenalin is released into the body in several ways. I will take them in turn.

Anticipation of Confrontation

When you anticipate confrontation the body slowly releases adrenalin, often over a long period of time. The slow release is not as intense as the fast release but, due to its longevity, it can wear and corrode the recipient. Things like the anticipation of having to talk in public, an exam, a big sales meeting, a forth-coming karate competition, or a planned confrontation with the partner/neighbour/boss will cause slow release up to months before the expected confrontation.

Fear of Consequence

When one anticipates the negative or positive consequences of confrontation before it even happens, the fear of that consequence, whether failure, success or humiliation, often forces the recipient to abort.

Pre-confrontation Fear

Psychologists like to call this adrenal dump; the bodyguards list it as the WOW factor. The fast release occurs when anticipation is not present, or a situation escalates unexpectedly fast, causing adrenal dump. This feeling is often so intense that the recipient freezes in the face of confrontation, the reasoning process mistaking it for sheer terror. This the most devastating of the three.

Adrenal dump often occurs when a confrontation arises that one was not prepared for; usually the same scenarios as those that cause slow release but with no anticipation. Perhaps you are in a meeting at work and are asked to address those present without any preparation, or you are confronted by your boss/neighbour/partner or an attacker without warning. It is often this first strike that starts the whole fear thing off so this is the one to watch out for.

It normally strikes when your mental guard is down, perhaps when you have been overworking or overthinking. This is your first opportunity to stop the fear from becoming fully-fledged. As soon as the feelings sweep over you, accept them without panic, let the fear-wave go in and out, don't tense, don't panic, examine the feelings and do not recoil or try and run from them. Whatever you do, don't panic, this is precisely the thing that will perpetuate fear.

It is so hard at times, I know. Almost the second you feel fear you have that dread of a reoccurrence and the questions start to race around your mind, 'Why is this happening to me, why am I so scared, why can't it just go away?' Don't allow yourself any self-pity, I have been here very many times, so I understand that it can be difficult. Your tendency is to try and fight it, and there is a part of you that just wants to scream, 'Get this out of me!'

As I said, panic perpetuates fear. Don't blame your body, it is only sending you adrenalin because it thinks you need it; it reads your panic as a tangible threat and so sends in the reinforcements. Of course, you don't need more adrenalin; you need less. But it is communicating this to a nervous system that is operated automatically. The very best way to do this is to accept the feelings of fear, deliberately stop yourself from panicking, no matter how tempted you are, and don't fight! Relax, accept it, feel it flowing through you, even challenge it to come in greater proportions and then just float above it.

panic, don't be blackmailed by it and don't dwell on irrational thoughts that trigger fear. Let them come into your mind and back out again. Don't connect to them in any way. Of course, if you have a decision to make then it needs to be made sooner because indecision is a big cause of stress and fear. Make your decision one way or another and see how the weight falls off you. Sometimes our fears are irrational and there is no actual decision to be made, other than accepting the fact that you are feeling fear and that you can deal with it for as long as it would like to stay. This is the way to get rid of it.

If you have a fear that is threatening you, perhaps you are worried that your business might fail, or you can't make the mortgage, or that your partner might stop loving you and run off with someone else, just think to yourself, 'Who cares? If it happens it happens, and if it does I'll deal with it. I don't care.' Keep saying that to yourself every time you feel threatened. Talk to yourself in your mind and tell the thoughts, 'Just do it, I can deal with that all day long.' Stop caring that the adrenalin pumps through your body. Accept it, and keep accepting it until it goes, which it will as soon as you start facing and accepting. When it comes, just float by it and let time pass.

Keep busy while you are feeling anxious. Often constant exposure to fear makes you very tense and can tire you out. The very last thing you want to do is be busy, but busy is the best way to be because it occupies your mind and gives it a rest from fearful thoughts. Be around people; company is one of the best ways of taking your mind away from your stress.

Physical Reactions to Adrenalin

These are some natural bodily reactions to adrenalin:

Pre-fight Shakes
Your legs, and possibly other limbs, may shake uncontrollably.

Dry Mouth
Your mouth may become dry and pasty.

Voice Quiver
Your voice may acquire a nervous and audible tremor.

Tunnel Vision
On the positive side, tunnel vision enhances visual concentration. Its negative by-product is the blinkering of peripheral vision.

Sweaty Palms and Forehead
The palms of the hands and forehead often sweat profusely.

Nausea
Adrenalin may cause vomiting, or the feeling of wanting to vomit.

Bowel Loosening
The recipient may experience constant urges to use the toilet.

Severe Reactions to Adrenalin

'Yellow' Fever
Adrenalin, certainly adrenal dump, evokes feelings of helplessness and abject terror. Fear of confrontation may bring on an extreme feeling of depression and foreboding. Tears may also occur. If you need to cry then have a good blub, it is an excellent release. Many people, especially men, are ashamed to cry, as though in

crying they are giving in. Crying is good; it can make you
lot lighter, so if you feel the need just do it. Again, don't latch o
to anything, and don't panic. All these feelings are a usual part of prolonged stress; when the mind is tired and the guard is down even the slightest thing can make you feel emotional.

Think of your mind as a tired muscle that needs feeding and resting to restore its full strength. To restore it, make sure that you eat well, even and especially when you don't feel like eating (one of the horrible side effects of fear is often lack of appetite). Also, get plenty of rest at night (you may not be able to sleep that soundly but you can still read or practise relaxation and mediation to give your body and mind a rest), and keep busy during the day.

Time Distortion

Many report that a confrontation seems to last an eternity, when in reality it may have only lasted a few minutes. During confrontation, time can appear to stand still; one minute often feeling like one hour. Paradoxically, many have said in retrospect, 'It all happened so fast.'

When interviewing James, the victim of an assault, he initially told me that he was attacked without warning. After talking to him at some length it turned out that, between first seeing his attackers and the attack itself, there was a time lapse of eleven seconds, this being originally lost to time distortion.

Restless Nights

Many suffer from restless nights when experiencing slow release and aftermath. This can often be one of the most upsetting aspects of prolonged fear or anxiety. You might a good night's sleep is impossible, and yet the daytime. It all adds to the fear because, become fearful about not sleeping; perhaps o bed at night. And if that's not bad enough you might wake up early in the morning with that dread hanging over you.

By being busy in the day you will find sleep easier at night. If you do find yourself lying there unable to get off to sleep, don't fret even if you feel like it, just practise some relaxation techniques. Breathe deeply through your nose and fill your lungs until your abdomen rises (about five times) and tense and relax each muscle in turn from your toes to your head.

Similarly, if you wake early in the morning and it is too early to rise (better to rise than to lie and ferment), practise relaxation, calm your mind and face and accept the feelings of fear without latching on to them. One of the things I always do if I find myself in this position is to plump up my pillows, switch on a lamp and read something inspiring. When you start to read you often find yourself drifting off to sleep without thinking.

If you wake in the morning and that dread hits you, instantly relax and talk yourself through it. Face it, accept it, let the wave go through and out and notice it as it does. Don't allow any feelings of panic to ensue. You may have had a great day and a good sleep and think that you are over it and then suddenly when you wake the feeling is back. The first thing you tend to think is, 'oh no, not again' as though a relapse is on its way. It isn't. The key is to not allow any thoughts of this into your mind. Go through the same procedure of facing and accepting and letting time pass.

No Appetite

When you are stressful or fearful your appetite tends to lessen, often resulting in weight loss, especially with slow release and aftermath. It is another upsetting aspect of fear. But it is so vital to eat, even and especially when you don't feel like it. Your body needs all the nourishment it can get; so eat, even take extra vitamins, feed your body and mind and make sure you eat the lot, right down to the last bit. The fuel is vital so don't worry that the food is having to be almost forced down and not enjoyed; eat for fuel. The sooner you get back to proper eating the sooner you will get past this thing. So fuel the journey.

Increased Heart Rate

Due to the turbodrive of adrenalin the heart rate often increases to what the recipient may feel is an abnormal level. Some may even experience chest pains as a result of tenseness in the pectoral region.

Depression

As a result of all the inner turmoil brought on by anticipation, depression often occurs. This is merely the result of a tired mind. Let the mind rest by keeping busy and, where necessary, making a decision to take away the inner turmoil. Make a decision one way or another and the mind will stop overworking. Start resting and of course the mind will regain its strength.

These are not the only bodily reactions to adrenalin, but they are certainly the main ones. Other reactions may occur as a direct result of confrontation.

All of the foregoing feelings are usual, if not exaggerated when in a stressed condition. Face, accept and ignore them, let them sweep through you and remember that they can't harm you in themselves. It is only when you panic that they perpetuate. The sooner you accept them the sooner they will disappear. The very moment you face and accept the feeling of fear without panic is the very second that you are on the way to recovery. This is the vital step. Facing and accepting, not panicking. They are all part and parcel of adrenal reaction and, though unpleasant, quite natural. The feelings cannot hurt or harm you and they do lessen in intensity as you become more exposed to them.

'The only thing we have to fear is fear itself.'

Franklin D Roosevelt

Chapter Two

The First Step

Even a journey of one thousand miles begins with a first step. The first step with fear is self-honesty. Many people never overcome their fears because they are afraid to admit them. Possibly they are embarrassed, even ashamed to admit their supposed failings, perhaps believing that others may think them weak for harbouring such fears. In reality it is truly a strong person who can be honest with themselves. I know; I spent years lying to myself, and being very unhappy as a direct result. Even an alcoholic cannot begin treatment until he first admits that he is an alcoholic.

The feeling of fear is as natural as the feelings of hunger and thirst and of wanting to use the toilet. I never met anyone that felt embarrassed or ashamed because they felt hungry, or thirsty or because they needed to use the loo.

I have met and worked with many people who told me that they felt no fear. They all turned out to be either very misguided or blatant liars. Saying that you don't feel fear is the same as saying that you don't feel hunger, thirst, love or hate. Everyone feels emotion and fear is one of the most powerful and primeval of emotions.

Fear is triggered by the anticipation of confrontation and is nature's way of helping us to survive life or death situations. Of course, confrontation is no longer the one-dimensional fight or flight scenario it was in bygone years. If a sabre-toothed tiger attacked you, you had two options. Your first option was always flight when possible and when this was not an option you had to fight for your life.

Confrontation in the twentieth century is rather more perplexing and in our cosmopolitan society there is a complicated paradox where, at once, both fight and flight are largely unacceptable. We are taught from primary school level that fighting is wrong whilst at the same time we are seen as cowards if we do not fight back against our adver-saries.

The body and mind are constantly at moral loggerheads. Physical instinct tells us to run or fight for survival; morality and contemporary peer pressure say 'don't fight!' whilst at the same time reminding us to stand up for ourselves. Even the law punishes us for our instincts, when we may only be defending our loved ones or ourselves.

On a subconscious level it seems the brain cannot distinguish between varying kinds of confrontation. If we anticipate a tangible confrontation, where the possible outcome may be a fight, the brain triggers adrenalin to aid response. If we anticipate an intangible confrontation, where there is no possibility of a physical outcome, such as a school exam, driving test, a speech or a showdown with the boss, the brain still releases adrenalin to aid response. Often, due to the nature of the confrontation, the adrenalin is not utilised and lies dormant in the body only to be released when someone cuts you up in the car or your child innocently spills a drink on the carpet.

Admitting your fears is often a very personal issue, perhaps not something that you would want to tell the whole world about. That's OK. Telling others is not always important, self-honesty is though.

People will often say, 'I'm not afraid of it [whatever 'it' may be], I just don't want to do it.' As a younger person I would always convince myself that I wasn't afraid of karate competitions, I just wasn't interested in competing. If that was really the case it would have been fine. In reality I found even the thought of competing nerve-racking and would experience slow release adrenalin up to a couple of months before the contest. This long-term anticipation would cause me sleepless nights and reduce my appetite. Lack of good food and sleep caused weight loss and depression. All of a sudden I was on a downward spiral, anticipation triggering many negative bodily reactions. The fact that I wasn't sleeping and eating would make me feel worse because, as I saw it, if I wasn't sleeping and eating then I must really have a problem.

The lack of food and sleep would also make me exhausted and being constantly tired lowered my defences, leaving me at the mercy of Mr. Negative, my inner opponent, who constantly told me how weak I was and how I couldn't handle the situation. Eventually I would get so down about the whole thing that I would ring up my instructor and make up some silly excuse as to why I couldn't enter the competition (I will talk more about the inner opponent in a later chapter).

This scenario is probably familiar to many: how often have you avoided certain scenarios due to the discomfort of anticipation, and then made up an excuse to cover your avoidance?

Admitting your fears is the first and foremost step in overcoming fear. Without self-honesty you are not even on the first rung of the ladder, nor will you ever be if you can't be honest with yourself.

It is also important not to kid yourself by saying, 'When I feel a little better about myself I'll do it.' 'When I'm a little fitter I'll enter a contest.' 'When I've got a little more money in the bank I'll start my own business.' And when you have enough money in the bank, 'I don't feel right yet, as soon as I do I'll go out on my own.'

There will always be a good excuse not to confront, always a good reason not to start, stop, leave or fight. It is worth remembering that it will be hard. If it was easy everyone would be a black belt in karate, a successful businessman, a confident person, have a great physique, hold a top job, drive a dream car and live with a perfect partner.

If you want success, in whatever form that may take, NOW is the time to start, not tomorrow, not next week, not on New Year's Day: now. Any delay always hints to me of a lack of commitment. Whoever you want to be, wherever you want to go, whatever you want to achieve can be done, but only you can do it. I can't give it to you and neither can anyone else. What I can do, however, is show you the way, so as to make the journey a little easier.

Chapter Three

A Few Home Truths

'If you know the time and place of the attack you can plan your defence from a hundred miles away.'

Sun Tzu

Before engaging a challenge and before setting out on any journey it is best to make plans.

There will be difficult times along the way but understanding this at the onset will lessen the shock impetus of any setbacks. The journey itself is where the real learning takes place. Here are a few truths to be remembered:

1) As long as you continue to learn and grow, fear will never go away.

You will overcome many different fears en route and these will bring higher self-esteem and a desensitisation to adrenalin. However, each time you approach a new situation at higher levels and each time you find yourself in unfamiliar circumstances you will feel fear again. Each new and subsequent fear will be more easily defeated because the techniques and confidence you have learned en route will serve you in good stead.

2) The only way to overcome the fear of doing something is to go out and do it.

You can sit in the classroom all day long talking about different aspects of your particular fear and how you're going to overcome them, what a great life you will have thereafter and the wonderful things that you want to achieve, but at the end of the day you won't learn to swim until you immerse yourself in the water. In other words, the only way to practise is to confront. No confrontation, no desensitisation. There are those who stay up all night dreaming about it and there are those who stay up all night doing it. Don't talk the talk when you can walk the walk.

Having said that, I have found that knowledge itself sometimes dispels fear to such an extent that confrontation is no longer a necessity. The more you understand and can learn about your particular fear the better; if it doesn't dispel it completely it will at least make it easier to confront. As they say, 'You cannot destroy what you cannot create.'

3) One of the best ways to feel better and get stronger is to go out and do it.

Everywhere I go I am confronted by people who are going to do this and going to do that. Every time I'm in the pub I'm told by beer guzzlers about great plans that are going to be realised, starting first thing tomorrow/next week/next year. Dreams that disappear next morning when sobriety arrives with a headache. Ironically, a lot of these talkers really do have the potential to realise all of their dreams if only they had the courage and conviction. I know many people in my own life who have bags of potential but they fail to utilise any of it for whatever reason and settle instead for the safe-bet life of mediocrity.

4) Everyone feels fear, especially in unfamiliar territory.

As a young person, frightened by my own shadow, I always felt that I was the only one that felt 'this scared'. This thought never ceased to spiral me down into ever-increasing misery. The greatest revelation for me was the fact that everyone felt the same in confrontational circumstances, though few of the people I spoke to in the early days would admit it. Do as I did and take great solace in the fact that we all feel the same. Some of the most successful people in the world started out as mentally weak and fearful people.

One of my friends, an SAS soldier and veteran of the Iranian Embassy siege, spent the first year of his Army life as a frightened, bullied sixteen-year-old. I asked him, out of all the life-threatening situations that he found himself in, which was the hardest to overcome. You may find it surprising to hear that, in his opinion, the bravest thing that he ever did was to confront a bully when he was sixteen years old, probably because it was his first step into the fear syndrome. Using this early lesson as a catalyst, he later joined the SAS and became one of the world's elite soldiers, facing death on a daily basis.

5) It gets easier.

The hardest step is often the first step. The first step is the decision to start, the decision not to take second place, the decision to fight back. Once you have made that decision you are halfway there. The beauty of it all is that once you have started and got a few successes under your belt you really start to enjoy the challenge. It is a little like the guys on the World's Strongest Man contest pulling trucks. Getting the truck started is a real toil, but once they build momentum it becomes easier and easier. It is a lot easier to keep momentum than to start it.

6) Living with fear is probably more painful than confronting fear.

I personally found that living with my fears was a lot more painful than actually confronting them. Your life and your potential are severely restricted when you live with fear, but to confront your fears is to enhance your life and expand your potential. When I was living under the dominion of my fears I felt imprisoned, and the decision to confront and overcome them was like the cell doors opening.

When I was scared and doing nothing about it my life seemed empty and limited by the walls of those fears, but when I went into action with a plan of attack my life suddenly became exciting and prosperous. The more I got into it the more I realised that there was nothing I couldn't do if I really wanted to.

Whatever the mind of man can conceive he can achieve.

The following short extract is taken from my autobiographical book *Watch My Back* and tells a little of my early journey.

All my early life, certainly from the age of eleven, I was plagued by a fear of fighting and confrontations. My mind was weak and constantly under attack from fears too powerful to defend against. Doubtless I was not on my own in this respect, but at the time I felt I was, so I could take no solace in the former. What I found to my distaste was not 'being scared' but the thought of having to live under its dominion for the rest of my life.

Many's the time I found myself sneaking out of the school's back entrance to avoid my would-be antagonists waiting for me at the front, and running off to the sanctuary of short-sightedness and ignorance only to wake up the next morning with fear and worry ever growing at the thought of having to go back to school and face 'the enemy' again, often having to go under the protective wing of my dad.

I vividly remember one Christmas morning sitting in my bedroom and crying, worrying about going back to school in two weeks' time, and the misery that would then ensue, and my elder brother coming in and asking me what was wrong. I shrugged my shoulders, too ashamed to admit my weakness. My whole childhood was marred by such incidents: these sad, scared, worried feelings came and went at will – I was at the mercy of my own mind.

In later years, and through my searching and experimenting, I learned that the explosion inside my stomach that I had once took for sheer terror and had struggled so long with was the adrenalin build-up, or the fight or flight syndrome; a chemical release from the adrenal gland that hits and goes through the bloodstream like a speeding tube train, preparing the body for fight or flight. It makes you temporarily stronger and faster and partially anaesthetises you from pain. The more dangerous the situation, the bigger the build-up and adrenalin release; the bigger the release the better you perform. But by the same count the bigger the build-up and release the harder it is to control, i.e. the easier it is for you to bottle out.

Cus Damatio once said that the feeling of fear is as natural as the feeling of hunger and thirst or of wanting to use the toilet. When you're hungry you eat. When you're thirsty you drink, and so it should be with the feeling of fear. You shouldn't panic under it, you should harness and then utilise it. So my goal became to control and master fear, rather than to erase it.

Now came the hard part, putting theory into practice. I needed exposure to stressful situations in a bid to conjure up fear in the hope that in confronting that fear I would become desensitised to it, 'confrontation, desensitisation', if you like. How to go about it though? I couldn't just go out and look for trouble – that would be going against the strict moral and ethical codes of karate, and also the law of karma, 'A good for a good, and a bad for a bad'.

The only way I could find round this was 'bouncing' in the Coventry pubs and nightspots. But I had to ask myself if I could hack it: Coventry seemed more famous those days for the monopoly it held on violence than for its three spires and cathedral. I was riddled with self-doubt. What if I got hammered? What if my bottle went? In the end the thought of living with my fears seemed to me to be worse than the fear of getting beaten up, in that the former was long-term, and the latter short-term. So began my term of office 'on the door'.

Please don't take this out of context, not everyone has a fear of fighting or a violently confrontational situation. What you fear may vary from spiders to a first speech; the concepts of overcoming those fears, however diverse they may appear, are the same, as I shall go into a little later.

Chapter Four

What Are You Afraid of?

This question should not be taken too literally, though the literal answer should already have been sought. It is one thing to admit your fears and quite another to analyse why you are afraid.

Your fear of making a big business decision may be due to a fear of failure; if the decision is a wrong one you may lose money, even your business. Your fear may be of success. If you make the right decision and your business doubles its turnover, could you cope with the extra workload that it would generate, taking in more stock, taking on more staff, generally taking more risks?

Similarly, a judo practitioner is scared of taking his black belt. Why? He may fear failure. If he fails the grade he may be embarrassed, he may feel that he loses the respect of his colleagues. The failure of one grading, especially the prestigious black belt, may force him to give up hope and stop training.

He may also fear success. If he passes he will be looked up to by those of a lower grade, this will give him added pressure that perhaps he feels he can't cope with. He may fear getting injured or ridiculed. As a black belt he may have to take on extra responsibilities at the club where he trains, they may even ask him to teach. As a brown belt he feels comfortable but as a black belt he may feel pressured.

Learning to swim as a child I can vividly remember the first time the teacher put me in the big group at the deep end of the pool. Now, in the shallow end I could swim up and down all day long. I felt safe because if things ever got a little too much for me, if I felt tired and wanted a rest, I knew I could place my feet on the floor at any time.

When the teacher put me in the deep end I became frightened because, whilst I knew I could swim, I was worried that if anything went wrong or I wanted a rest I couldn't. The water was too deep for me to touch the floor. Subsequently, I couldn't swim in the deep end.

Many people feel this about confronting their fears. They feel that if they fail they may be ridiculed in front of their peers, and they wouldn't be able to handle it. If they succeed they feel that they would be out of their depth and they wouldn't be able to handle that either.

I always believe that there is no such thing as failure: the fact that you have tried already makes you a success. The fact that you have tried also puts you well and truly on the first rung of the ladder to success. Of course there will be many people on the sidelines ready to see you fall, that's life, but ask yourself this. Who are these people? They are mere spectators in life whilst you are a player. You are not a failure because you do not make it, you are a success because you tried.

Try to analyse why it is you have a fear of something and then come to terms with it. The three golden words to help you cope with the consequences of your actions, whether they are successful or not are, *I'll handle it*.

If I'm a success and I get added pressure, I'll handle it.

If things don't work out, I'll handle it.

If I lose my job, I'll handle it.

If I change jobs and don't like the new job, I'll handle it.

If my partner leaves me, I'll handle it.

The Worst-case Scenario

Look at the worst-case scenario and tell yourself that if it happens *I'll handle it*. And then set about making plans so that the worst-case scenario never happens.

No matter what it is that you fear, at the end of it will be *I won't be able to handle it.*

If I go to the dentist and he doesn't use enough painkillers, it'll hurt and I won't be able to handle it.

If I take that new job I might not be up to it and be ridiculed, I couldn't handle that.

If I give up my job and home to work or travel abroad and it doesn't work out, I couldn't handle it.

If I buy myself that new car and then lose my job I wouldn't be able to pay for it. I couldn't handle that.

A good example of this is an incident that happened to me after a particularly nasty incident in *Watch My Back*. After a battle with some soldiers, myself and the doormen were herded into the manager's office, by the police, to watch the incident as recorded on the clubs CCTV.

> *Three policemen, two managers and four doormen squeezed into the tiny manager's office that had been tidied up especially. I tried to keep an 'I'm innocent, officer' look on my face, but it wasn't easy knowing what was on film. Cigarette smoke herded the air and daggered my eyes. My brain buzzed and busied itself trying to analyse and assess the situation ahead of me. No one was speaking, all eyes hit the TV screen as it crackled into life. Dave, the ultra thin, bespectacled manager, who was continually pushing the specs back up his nose, wound the tape forward to where it all began. I prayed that a miracle had occurred and I was off camera, or that the tape would suddenly, mysteriously break down. Dream on: I knew that I was going to be tonight's celluloid star. 'Play' was pressed and the silent movie began its recall. I hoped it was going to be kind to me.*

Initially it was. It showed us diligently trying to stop the quarrelling and then being attacked from behind by the unscrupulous, unprovoked soldiers as they left the club.

'Stop!' demanded the hefty sergeant, whose clean cut, smart features put you more in mind of a bank manager than a policeman. My heart missed a beat. Dave dutifully put the tape on pause at the sergeant's bidding. The sergeant then pointed ominously to the screen.

'Who's that?'

His finger aimed at the dozen on screen, frozen in a second of muted, vehement viciousness, but more accurately at myself. The panic I felt inside was like I have never felt before. It engrossed my body like a rapidly enlarging growth that was forcing all the self-control in my whole being outwards. I breathed in deeply, controlling it, captaining it, but still it pushed out-wards, fighting against me, hacking at my weakness with the sword of self-doubt. My inner opponent went to work, 'you'll get locked up – there will be comebacks – you'll go to prison for this, PRISON, PRISON, PRISON!' The ship of my moral fibre was under the threat of mutiny from the minority 'yellow crew' (inner opponent) within me. I cracked the whip of self-control and herded the craven in me back to captivity.

'That's me.'

I answered the sergeant's question, hiding my inner turmoil. His eyes searched mine for the weakness that he wouldn't find. It was under lock and key.

'You used a duster,' he challenged.

'No, I never used anything,' I lied, meeting his challenge.

He by-passed my denial.

'That's out of order son,' he said condemningly.

The silence rang in my ears for a long, long second (time distortion), broken by the whirl of the video as the sergeant pressed play on the video and all eyes left me for the screen. The voice of ill reason (my inner opponent again) started again in my head. 'You're scared. You're finished. Admit it, they've got you, they've got you. Give in, give in. You're weak, you're weak, you're not strong enough.' Each tried to hook on to a ledge of weakness, but I ignored the voice and countered consciously, 'I'm not scared. They haven't got me. I'm not finished. I'll never give in. I can handle it.' Then I challenged my own mind (my inner opponent), 'Give it your best shot, I can handle anything that you throw at me.' I knew from experience that your own mind can be your worst enemy and that as soon as you give in, even a little bit, to these thoughts, they grow stronger and stronger, feeding on each little victory, making you weaker and weaker. The key was to fight back and not listen to the voice. That was the only way to stop it.

In this case the worst-case scenario was that I could go to prison but I told myself that if that happened *I could handle it*.

People feel that by taking chances they are risking security. Security is knowing in your mind that, if it comes to the worst, you can handle it.

I invested my last few pounds on self-publishing one of my earlier books. I was really worried that if it didn't work out I would lose my savings so before I committed the money to the book I told myself that if it didn't work and the book flopped, I could handle it.

Remember, ships are safe in the harbour, but that is not what ships were made for.

You need to take chances if you want to expand. I read an apt saying in Susan Jeffers' book *Feel the Fear, and Do It Anyway*, 'If you always do what you've always done, you'll always get what you've always got.'

Life is like a huge supermarket full of all the things we want, but it is no different to an ordinary supermarket where you have to pay for the goods. The only difference is that in the supermarket of life the currency is time, dedication, commitment and calculated risk. All the things are in there for anyone who is willing to pay the price; if you're not you'll always be a window shopper.

I worked hard to become a qualified wrestling coach and one of my friends said he'd love to be one too, as though the achievement were beyond him. 'You can be,' I told him, emphatically. 'Just give me your Fridays for the next year, some dedication and a bit of discomfort, and you can be a wrestling coach.' He really did want to be a wrestling coach, but not that much. Like most people – and like myself as a younger man – he wanted something for nothing. What he failed to understand is that the certificate would mean nothing on its own, the real goal is the journey and the character you develop during that year of commitment and dedication.

The *If Only* Game

Similarly, many people talk about the fact that they would love to do this, be that, go there, and achieve that. They talk from a negative viewpoint as if none of it is realistically possible. It is. When I tell them this they invariably reel out a long list of if onlys. They play the *if only* game.

If only I wasn't so busy I could study for that doctorate.

If only I didn't have a mortgage and a family I'd take a chance on running my own business.

If only I wasn't so committed here I'd sell up and travel the world.

If only I had the energy I'd study a different art to make my own more complete.

If only… if only… if only. If only people would stop making excuses they would do something with their lives other than watch them go by. No matter what the circumstances there will always be an *if only*, especially if you are looking for one. If only is often just another way of saying *I'm scared to do it.* I should know, I have played the if only game enough times myself. Packing up your job, selling your house and then travelling the world is not easy and there are a myriad of *if onlys* that stop thousands of people from doing it every day. But there are some that it does not stop. There are dozens of *if onlys* that stop people from studying part-time to become lawyers, for instance, but Richard, a friend of mine, managed to do it whilst working two other jobs.

I've lost count of the number of people I know who would love to travel to America to train with some of the world's greatest martial artists. The *if onlys* would never allow it, though it never stopped Rick Young from travelling to the US twice a year and becoming a world-renowned martial artist. And, at the time, Rick worked as a postman in the day and taught martial arts classes in the evenings, so his *if onlys* must have been tremendous.

John Fenton, now a multi-millionaire, was brought up as a normal working class boy, but he didn't allow the *if onlys* to stop him becoming what he is today.

Bob Spour always wanted to be a lovey so he gave up everything; work, money, the lot, to go to full-time drama school and become an actor.

Mike Tyson, probably the most talked about boxer this century, was plagued as a young man from fears much greater than himself and had a mountain of *if onlys*, but he didn't let them stop him becoming a legendary sportsman. If you really want something then nothing will get in your way; if you are afraid for whatever reason the mind will manufacture a thousand feasible *if onlys* to stop you in your tracks.

So make sure that you can deal with the *if onlys* right from the outset. Accept the risks that are involved. There will always be risks, if there were no risks there would be no problem and everyone would be living happy and successful lives. It is our fears that stop us from achieving our goals.

Chapter Five

Comfort Zones

Most people find their own little niche in life, a comfort zone within which they feel safe. Whilst inside the parameters of their comfort zones they can pretty much do as they please without too much discomfort, but as soon as they venture outside of those walls the fear starts.

Your comfort zone may be your job, your relationship, your martial arts club, your lifestyle, or for someone phobic it may be the confines of your house. Your comfort zone may be anything on ground level if you are terrified of heights, or being with less than five people if you're scared of crowds; the list can go on and on. As a young person my fear was life itself. I was afraid of change.

My Marriage

Whilst my marriage was not happy, it was safe. I did not love the person I was with but was too scared to be without a partner.

If I split from my wife I feared I'd lose access to my children and have nowhere to live. My self-esteem was so low I felt that I might not get another girlfriend, I was worried that someone else would want my wife if I left (even though I didn't want her myself), and afraid that I might leave and then realise that I really did love her after all and then she wouldn't have me back. I was afraid that the whole issue would grow out of my control and make me depressed, and that I wouldn't be able to handle it.

My Job

Quite frankly my job was abysmal, I hated every minute of the seven years I worked as a chemical plant operator, but hey, it was safe, and jobs like that aren't that easy to come by (the best move I ever made was the day that I left). This of course was underlined by all my workmates and many of my family members who felt that they just had to tell me how lucky I was to have such a good job.

I was scared to leave because I felt that there were too many risks involved. What if I didn't find another job? I wouldn't be able to pay the mortgage, they might take the house off me. What would become of the family, my poor kids, without a home? I'd be a failure and everyone would say 'I told you so.'

I even worried about changes within the workplace. If someone new was taken on I would worry about whether or not I'd get along with them. What if they were objectionable people and the workplace became a hive of arguments? I couldn't handle that, arguing every day, that would make me depressed and I hate being depressed.

If I was asked to take on extra responsibility it would get me down because I feared that I might not be up to it, I might fail and be ridiculed.

What if I succeeded? The managers would be pleased with that success and probably give me more responsibility and then I'd be stuck with it forever.

I was afraid of failure and at the same time I was afraid of success; I was afraid of change and yet, paradoxically I was also afraid of no change which would mean I would be stuck in a bad job for the rest of my life.

The Goldfish Bowl Syndrome

People are a little like goldfish in that they will only grow as big as the bowl you place them in.

If you put a goldfish in a small bowl he would not grow, but put him in a big bowl and he will grow to accommodate it. If you put him in a pond he would expand yet again.

The goldfish bowl is our metaphoric comfort zone: to grow we have to continually extend the parameters of the bowl. Whilst this may be initially uncomfortable, it is the only way. Of course, with the bigger bowl comes greater responsibility but that is all part and parcel of expanding. If I farm one acre of land and decide to take on another acre I will get twice the crop. But twice the crop will mean twice the work and responsibility.

Pay-offs for not Confronting and Expanding

Expanding the comfort zone will add excitement and potential to your life, but not expanding means staying exactly where you are. The reason most people do not expand are the pay-offs. There are so called 'benefits' to just remaining where you are. Once you realise and accept this you will be ready to move.

1) Comfort Zone

The first pay-off for not confronting your fears and expanding is the comfort zone.

This is an empty threat that the mind will make to keep you from growing. *If you grow you'll lose your comfort zone.* You do not really lose the comfort zone because it is replaced by a new one, and when that is broken it will be replaced again and again. Nothing is really lost, but an awful lot is gained.

2) No Rejection

One of the major fears of expansion is rejection. Many people have an innate fear of being rejected, by potential employers, partners, workmates, peers or simply have a fear of being rejected by life. You may fear that your old friends will reject you because you become a success, or your new associates reject you for daring to succeed. If your family does not grow with you, you may feel that they will reject you for growing alone. Rejection is always a possibility.

When I left my job as a nightclub doorman and made a success of writing I was surprised to find that many of my old friends began to reject me. Perhaps they were envious of my success; perhaps they thought me pretentious for daring to try; maybe they felt betrayed that I had expanded when and where they dared not. Whatever the reason, the rejection was tangible and at first I found it very disconcerting, even discouraging. I also felt rejection as I tried to expand into new areas, many of my peers incredulous that I dared try to better myself and enter their world (I shall enlarge on this in a later chapter). It bothered me, until I realised that rejection was their problem and not mine and would only affect me if I let it.

My friends of old who rejected me were obviously not really friends, the acid test of my success had proved that. Those in front of me, who I looked upon as peers, were not worthy of the term, and if my success bothered them they were obviously insecure people who were on the way down and not up.

Rejection is a sign of other people's weaknesses and should not even be considered, only by-passed.

3) No Failure

Another negative pay-off is *if I don't try I can't fail.* The act of not trying is a failure on its own, so if you do not try you have failed to even get to the starting line. If you do try it means you have succeeded already.

The real battle is not with the elements, it is with yourself.

If you are frightened to enter a race in case you lose but enter the race anyway, whether you win the race or not is irrelevant because you have beaten yourself by entering against your own will.

Entering a marathon is a good example. The majority of people do not enter marathons to win but to complete the course and if and when they do they are elated simply because they have finished it. Some see success as the fact that they have beaten their own previous record.

A woman who had a fear of eating in busy restaurants finally decided to challenge her fear and, for the first time, arranged to visit a particularly busy restaurant that night with her husband. She managed to get right to the restaurant doors but, on hearing the hum of voices inside, could go no further and had to leave.

All the way home in the car she cried because she felt that she had failed, until her husband pointed out that reaching the restaurant doors was a great success because on previous attempts she had not even got to the stage of booking a table. Using this as a catalyst she was eventually able to completely confront her fears of busy restaurants once and for all.

A young child who walks for the first time is not a failure because he only takes two steps, he is a success because he has never walked before. He is not a failure when he walks only five steps, he is a success because, whilst five steps may not seem a lot, it is still three steps better than two.

Failure is a negative word that really should not exist. We probably learn more from a failure than a success, so in reality failure is just an alternative set of experiences. We learn how to succeed from success, we learn from failure how not to fail again and subsequently how to succeed. I have been down a few avenues that didn't work for me but the experience was invaluable, things were learned that could never have been learned in any other way. As they say, 'The man who has not made a mistake has not done anything.' Or as Billy Connolly said, 'That's why there is a rubber at the end of your pencil!'

4) You Can Handle It

'I might not be very happy with my lot, but at least I can handle it.' Many people feel that they can handle what they have now but taking on any more would be too much. You have to believe that you can handle more, tell yourself that you can or, again, growth will not be imminent. We are not talking about confronting all your fears at once and going from a goldfish bowl straight into a huge pond; that would be unrealistic and could cause disorientation. Rather we are talking about very gradual steps that will slowly but surely expand your comfort zone.

When I first started weight training I could bench press 60lb with a struggle, whilst my training partner could push an impressive 160lb. To me this seemed an impossible feat. If I had tried there and then to lift 160lb it would indeed have been impossible, but by pyramiding the weight, slowly increasing the amount I lifted over the next six months, expanding the physical comfort zone of how much I could lift by a few pounds at a time, I too was able to push 160lb and later as much as 250lb. Something that I would never have thought possible I now handled with ease.

My original physical comfort zone of 60lb became so light that it was not even heavy enough for me to use as a warm-up weight.

Similarly a shop-floor worker in a factory does not expect to go straight to company chairman. But he may go in very steady steps from labourer to machinist, then to shop-floor foreman, to senior foreman then management and later to company chairman.

So expand the comfort zone, find your feet, become orientated with the new altitude and then expand again. If the doubts about your ability to handle it come flooding in, tell yourself that you can and will handle it. Risk is the cavernous hole that lies between those that dream and those that do. If there were no risks there would be no point: everyone would have everything they wanted.

5) Security

Security is another pay-off for staying and not expanding, a little like myself when I worked at the chemical plant. I hated the job but the thought of losing my security by moving to a new and better job, by expanding my comfort zone, kept me glued to the spot, especially when this was underlined by those around me. Security is no more than being able to handle anything that life throws at you and if you expand your comfort zone at a gradual pace then your security need never be compromised anyway.

Many people spend their whole lives planning and saving for the rainy day that never comes, never really taking chances and never really enjoying what they have. Some end up dying with a lot of money in the bank having lived a relatively empty life.

I have a friend whose father was a little shy when it came to spending any of his hard-earned money. Even though he had plenty of it, he lacked many of the luxuries of life that he wanted because he daren't spend. He feared that spending would compromise his security.

When his son told him that he should enjoy his money he replied, 'When I die, you'll inherit all my money.' His son said, 'I don't want your money when you're dead, I want you to enjoy it now, while you're alive.' This obviously hit home because he went out the next day and bought his wife a new kitchen.

The Chinese say, 'If you earn two pennies, spend one on food to live and one on flowers to give you a reason to live.'

The *When* Complex

When I've got a safe amount of money in the bank I'll…

have the car that I've always wanted

take my dream holiday

buy a new kitchen

do a little less overtime

buy the Rolex watch that I've always said I'd buy when the money was there.

It's a cop-out. It's similar to saying, 'When I feel better about myself I'll confront my fears/finish the relationship/start the new relationship.'

When I'm a little fitter I'll join the gym

When I'm a little more financially secure I'll start my own business

When I'm more confident I'll join the karate/judo/boxing club.

When, of course, often never comes, or if it does it is extended with another *when.*

People fail to live for fear of risking their security so they end up unhappy and unfulfilled in a dingy but tight comfort zone. Paradoxically, many become very insecure in their secure units because they live in fear of external disruption like losing their jobs.

When you have come to terms with and can accept that there is far more to gain than there is to lose, expansion and confrontation become more viable concepts.

Chapter Six

Step Two

A lot of people do nothing about their fears simply because they do not know how. Even once they have analysed all we have covered in the previous chapters they still don't know how to go about conquering their fears.

In this chapter I should like to offer the reader a road map to help on the journey from pain to personal power. I know that some of you out there may be getting a little impatient and wanting me to cut to the chase. That would be very easy to do, it would also save me a lot of time, but, unfortunately it would not help you.

Like painting the woodwork in your house, priming and preparation are pivotal if a good and lasting job is to be achieved. If you prepare the surface and apply a good undercoat the glossing is so much easier and the finish so much more professional; if you don't prepare you only do half a job.

Here are a few things that people need to understand.

1) Planning to venture into a threatening situation

It is important that you have a game plan and definite, achievable goals. It's very easy to lose direction and energy if you haven't got a road map from where you are to where you want to go. When I travel from one city to another teaching, I always acquire directions; if I didn't I probably wouldn't get there, and if I did it would definitely take me a lot longer and I'd use up a lot more fuel.

In this case the road map would be from *how you feel and where you are now* to *how you want to feel and where you want to be at the end of the journey.* This can be achieved using the *fear pyramid* (detailed later).

My own game plan was to go from a position of personal weakness to a position of power by systematically confronting my fears, one by one, starting with my least fears and gradually building up to my bigger fears. I realistically saw myself, on my road map, as a weak person who was afraid of many things, especially my bodily reactions to confrontation and change. A person not in charge of his own life and therefore his own destiny.

My destination was personal power; at the end of my metaphoric journey I wanted to be in charge of me. I knew that real power was not in being able to get others to do what I wanted but rather to be able to get myself to do what I wanted. My goal therefore was to be able to live a brave and exciting life, where I was not under the dominion of every little fear that happened to pass by. My strategy was to do this by confronting and gaining exposure to my fears. What you might call paradoxical intention. After all, what we resist persists. My intention was not to try and find a route around fear – there isn't one – rather to go the direct route right through the heart of it.

So you need to know where you are now and where you want to be. A tangible goal will give you definite direction.

2) Coping with the anticipation of failure

From my experience, anticipation is usually far worse than confrontation. It is reported that ninety-five per cent of all the things we fear never happen, therefore ninety-five per cent of the time we are worrying for nothing. The way to deal with this is to take a close look at what failure is, and whatever it is, accept it. Tell yourself that *you can handle it*.

As I said before, risk is the cavernous hole between those that dream and those that do. It is risk that separates the talkers from the walkers, it sorts out the men from the boys. Risk is the barrier that places ninety-five per cent of the success with five per cent of the populace, that five per cent being those that accept risk as part and parcel of confrontation.

Whenever I am confronted by a particularly pressing situation, whether it is taking a risk with an investment or dealing with a threatening situation, I look at the worst-case scenario. If I make this decision/take on this challenge/confront my fear/ leave my partner or job, what is the worst thing that could happen? Whatever it is, I tell myself that *I can handle that.*

If I lose money or even my business taking a chance on an investment, I'll handle it.

If I meet that monster on the common and I get a good hiding, I can handle that.

I remember once having to appear on a popular TV programme to do a national phone-in on self-protection with me as the expert answering the viewers' questions and offering advice. Now, I've appeared frequently on the TV and I usually cope very well with it. However, on this occasion I was expected to appear for some fifteen minutes, live. In fifteen minutes it would be very easy to trip up and make myself look an absolute fool. It was made worse by the fact that everyone around me felt it was their job to tell me how silly I would look if I did trip.

Initially it all got to me and I started listening to these, probably well intentioned mates. Eventually I came to my senses and had a good think about the show. I made plans to study my subject well beforehand and I told myself that if everything went wrong and I looked silly in front of the whole nation, I'd handle it. If looking silly was the worst thing that could happen, I could handle that standing on my head.

I also told my friends and associates not to talk to me if all they had to offer was negativity. I told them that if I did look daft at least I was out there having a go, I had already succeeded where they had failed by actually appearing on the show. Once I had accepted that I could handle the worst-case scenario my fears disappeared and the show was a success (even if I say so myself).

So, look at the worst thing that could happen and tell yourself, *I can handle it*. Also remember that there is no such thing as failure, only different experiences, all of which offer a lesson.

3) Enlisting the help of those who are sympathetic

Don't hesitate to enlist the help of others, especially those who understand your dilemma. I have many students who ring me on a regular basis for help, support and an occasional dose of inspiration. A problem shared is a problem halved.

If you have no one close to you who can help, join a support group or seek inspiration or answers from books and tapes. I always used to read books that inspired me to succeed, later to listen to inspirational audio tapes or music. Inspiration is a particularly important aspect that needs topping up daily. Every time you feel a little down or as though you can't go on, listen to a tape or read a book to kick-start your flagging ego.

4) Dealing with the unpredictable behaviour of others

Parallel to this, you should also try to avoid negative people who, for whatever reason, do not want you to succeed. People can often be very fickle, even those who you think are your friends can suddenly become messengers of foreboding. I always make a point of avoiding these people or simply taking them to one side and asking them why they insist on putting me off.

There is no need to fall out with these people, just ask them, 'Why are you being so negative?' or, 'If you can't offer me encouragement I'd rather you kept your thoughts to yourself.' More than anything do not take in any of the negativity, you have to learn to close your ears to these types of people.

I remember a friend of mine actually scoffing when I told him that I was going to try and become a full-time writer, he more or less told me not to get above my station. Others said 'Grow up' and 'people like us [working class people] don't write books.'

These were just two of several of my so-called friends, and I don't mind telling you that their comments cut me to the quick. Those who refused to grow with me are still where they were when I left them. Sometimes if people will not grow with you, you have to leave them behind (more on this subject later).

5) Finding alternatives to running away from fear

There is more than one way to skin a cat, as the old saying goes. If a direct assault on your fear is too much to contemplate, break down the fear into smaller components that are a little more manageable or try to come in at a different angle. Breaking down the fear into smaller components (to be detailed later) can mean confronting manageable fragments of the fear until the whole unit is confronted and overcome.

One of my early fears was of spiders and rather than just jumping in the deep end and picking up a spider (which can work well for some) I spent a little time studying it from a distance. I gradually got closer and closer, touching the spider with an extension, a piece of stick or a pencil, so that I could get used to the sudden movements of the spider. Later still I could touch it with my finger. Eventually I was able to pick up the spider and let it crawl over my hand without any fear or discomfort.

Coming in from a different angle may mean, for instance, building confidence by talking to someone who has already trodden the same path and overcome the fear, or even watching someone else do what you are afraid to do.

When I went to buy my first new car I had a terrible fear that by getting the car through my business and on finance I would be getting out of my depth. I worried that I could not really afford the car, even though I knew that I could; I worried that my business might fail and I would not be able to afford the repayments. For some perverse reason I also felt that I was, in some way, not worthy of such an expensive car. Rather than directly confront my fear by going out and purchasing the vehicle I phoned up an associate, someone who was familiar with my business and who had had several expensive company cars over the years, and asked his opinion.

I started the conversation negatively by telling him that I wasn't going to get the car because I couldn't afford it. Without any hesitation he told me that I should go right out and get the car. 'You and I both know that you can afford it, and if you don't get it now you'll always regret it,' he said emphatically. Of course I knew that he was right and that I was worrying for nothing. Speaking to him gave me the confidence to go out and get the car and I never did regret it, nor was there ever a time when I could not afford the payments. Having said that, if the business couldn't stand the payments I would have been unwise to make the purchase.

Sun Tzu said that before you wage war you should first count the costs. Count the costs and make sure that you are ready to handle the outcome, whatever it may be.

Draw up your road map and check out the worst-case scenarios at the beginning of the journey, and always tell yourself that no matter what happens, you'll handle it.

Chapter Seven

The Inner Opponent

The ugly handmaiden of fear is the omniscient Mr Negative. General Sun Tzu called him the inner opponent, Susan Jeffers called him the chatterbox, I call him Mr Negative.

The inner opponent is the negative voice that perches on your shoulder and tells you that you're frightened, scared or that you can't handle the situation. Many people are not beaten by their fear but by their own minds. A negative notion that latches on to a subconscious insecurity soon grows into a monstrously big inner opponent that forces people to acquiesce a lot sooner that they should. The inner opponent is responsible for beating more people than any tangible or intangible fear. It is fair to say that if you cannot beat the man on the inside then you cannot beat the man on the outside.

I remember a wonderful story about a wrestler who was travelling by train from Glasgow to London to wrestle the legendary Bert Asarati, renowned for 'hurting' his opponents. All the way down on the train journey the wrestler fought with his inner opponent who kept on reminding him of the prowess of Mr Asarati. Every time the train stopped at a station the wrestler's inner opponent tempted him to get off and go back to Glasgow. At each station the inner opponent got stronger and stronger, the wrestler's will getting weaker and weaker. By Birmingham the wrestler could stand no more. He got off the train and took the next train back to Glasgow. Mr Asarati received a note from the wrestler that said, 'Gone back to Glasgow, you beat me in Birmingham'.

His inner opponent defeated him hours before he was due to enter the ring.

This story will be familiar to many, only the opponent may not have been an eighteen stone wrestler, but a big business deal, the decision to change job/home/car/relationship, ask the boss for a rise, travel the world, start up a new business, expand an existing business. To the phobic it may have been leaving the house, going in a plane, travelling in a car, going in a lift or up an escalator.

Many are beaten before the fight by their own minds. Why? Because it takes no effort to think negative thoughts, the inner opponent will do that for you; to think positive thoughts however takes a lot of effort. This extract is from James Clavel's book *Shogun*:

> *'To think bad thoughts is really the easiest thing in the world. If you leave your mind to itself it will spiral you down into ever-increasing unhappiness. To think good thoughts, however, requires effort. This is one of the things that training and discipline are about. So teach your mind to dwell on sweet perfumes, the touch of silk, tender raindrops against the shoji, the tranquillity of dawn; then at length you won't have to make such an effort and you will be of value to yourself.'*

Left to its own devices the mind can be a self-detonating time bomb of negativity that will spiral you down into ever-increasing misery. Dealing with the inner opponent is firstly about understanding that everyone has an inner opponent (though very few come to terms with him) and understanding that we will never reach our full potential whilst he has the run of our heads. Mr Negative is very controllable, if you know how.

These are three ways that I have found successful in dealing with Mr Negative:

1) Thought Rejection

Reject the negative thoughts by completely ignoring them, not listening to anything that Mr Negative says, thus leaving him no mental ledge on which to perch.

This is harder than it seems and demands self-discipline. Negative thoughts have a habit of swimming into your mind, uninvited and at will. Don't have any of it. It is your mind, you are in charge. Occupy your mind by reading, listening to the radio, by keeping yourself busy, watching the box, anything to take your mind away from the negative thoughts. Don't give in and panic with the thoughts because that will cause them to multiply ten-fold and then twentyfold and before you know it your mind will be overrun by negative emotion that can quickly turn to depression. So just ignore them.

2) Thought Counter-attack

If you just can't ignore Mr Negative, try thought counter-attack (this is the method that I practise). Fight your inner opponent by countering every negative thought he throws at you with a positive thought of your own.

Mr Negative:	*You're scared.*
Your counter:	*No, I'm not scared.*
Mr Negative:	*You can't handle this situation.*
Your counter:	*Yes, I can handle this situation, I can handle anything.*
Mr Negative:	*You're out of your depth, you'll never cope.*
Your counter:	*I'm not out of my depth and I can cope, in fact I'll cope easily.*
Mr Negative:	*You'll fail and everyone will laugh.*
Your counter:	*If that's the worst that can happen, I can handle it.*

3) Repetitive Mantra

You can block out the negative thoughts with repetitive mantras.

I can handle it... I can handle it... I can handle it...

I'm in charge... I'm in charge... I'm in charge...

I'm not scared... I'm not scared... I'm not scared...

The list goes on and on. By countering your inner opponent you will erase the negative thoughts with the positive. You have to learn not to take any crap from the inner opponent and fight, tooth and nail, every time that he rears his ugly head. Watch out though, he can be a cheeky beggar and if you are not vigilant he will try to sneak in when you least expect it.

Even the feelings that accompany negativity can be countered with defiance. I always tell myself, 'Do your worst, I can handle it, I can handle twice what you're giving me.' The biggest fight is always with yourself and the more wins you get under your belt the stronger you become and the weaker your inner opponent becomes. Once you have the inner opponent under control you are well on the way.

Fight back negativity right from the outset. Each negative thought you allow to penetrate your psyche may and usually does erode a small part of your will until eventually you are defeated. I work on the premise that *negative begets negative, begets defeat*. As a parallel, *positive begets positive, begets victory.*

Your greatest enemy in times of adversity is your own mind. Tell your inner opponent that *you can handle it*.

Once you have come to terms with Mr Negative and have learned to accept fear as a friend, allow adrenalin the run of your body and don't allow yourself to panic. Knowledge is power. By understanding your own body, by understanding the mechanics of adrenalin and fear you can learn self-control. Panic is catalysed by ignorance; by not understanding your own body or its workings. Most people in most situations are not defeated by their fears; they are defeated by their own minds. Whilst the feeling of fear can be uncomfortable it cannot hurt you, it is a natural feeling that should be accepted without panic. There is no way around these feelings, everyone feels them, they are a part and parcel of adversity.

Chapter Eight

The Treatment

In brief and to be blunt, the best way to overcome a fear is to confront it. The process is called exposure therapy. By exposing yourself to the fear you become desensitised to it. Learning only takes place whilst you are actually inside the confrontational situation; the same way that you can only practise swimming whilst immersed in water.

The A, R and O Theory of Fear Control

My own theory of fear control, derived from many years of facing violence as a way of life in society's culture dish, the night-club, consists of giving adrenalin the run of your body until you are ready to channel it. A little like water that flows around a tank released with the turn of a tap. As a young person I was, unfortunately, at the mercy of my own adrenal gland; when the adrenalin flowed, I ran. I made the classic error of mistaking adrenalin for fear and thus thinking myself a coward. I also felt that I was the only person in the world who felt this way.

A, R and O? Accept, recognise and override. Accept fear into your body, recognise that it is adrenalin and then override it by dealing with the adversity. To stop the fear from perpetuating, kill negative thoughts as soon as they try to enter your mind.

The Cut Out Button

Generally the inner opponent does not allow us full control of our own minds, implanting thoughts that we would rather not be thinking. If it says Stop, we generally do just that; if it says, *Don't fight, you'll fail* generally we do not fight and subsequently fail by not trying.

The brain has been installed with an automatic 'cut out' button, built in by nature to protect the body and mind from burn-out.

Due to evolution (and a distinct lack of prehistoric animals in our everyday lives) and soft living this automatic cut out is often set at a very low tolerance point; the slightest hint of stress or pain and the brain cuts out, leaving us well short of our desired goal because we capitulate far too readily. This is why it is said that most people go to their graves with their best songs still in them.

Extending Cut Out

This cut out button can and has to be extended if we want to attain any measure of success in our lives (everybody's cut out point is set at a different tolerance and some people are gifted with a very high tolerance level). This is achieved simply by mastering the inner opponent and gradually stretching our own limits until we are at our full potential.

The Pain Barrier

Just past the cut out point for those who push through it is the infamous pain barrier. Extending or erasing the cut out point is the pot of gold at the end of the rainbow. This goal will not be acquired without an epic and arduous battle with your own mind. You must dare yourself to take the challenge. Remember the old adage of the SAS: Who dares wins.

To summarise: when you feel fear, recognise it as a nat
reaction to confrontation, accept its presence calml
panic, counter any negative thoughts and override them.

Adrenal Exposure

Pain, fear, exhaustion, boredom, low self-esteem and the inner opponent will all, at one time or another (or all together) gnaw away at your weaker links trying to make you quit, give in, surrender, capitulate. Overcoming and defeating these elements will greatly extend the cut out point and help you to develop a strong character, greatly heightening your self-esteem.

The Indomitable Spirit

It is eventually possible to completely erase the cut out point, where, in theory, you could find that nothing would be beyond achievement. This, though, is the singular most difficult goal to achieve, known as the elusive indomitable spirit. The more that you experience and confront the fear syndrome, the more desensitised you will become to it and the easier it will be to control and thus harness. The more that you confront and control, the stronger minded you will become. These exercises in confronting and controlling will build the mental muscle like a bar-bell and weights will build physical muscle. The same dictum 'no pain, no gain' is also appropriate.

This gained strength of mind will put your whole life into perspective: all of a sudden those mundane tasks at work or around the home become simple challenges by comparison. All are relegated to simple exercises in self-discipline; everything that life throws in your way become challenges that you no longer baulk at and nothing will seem beyond the purlieus of your mental capacity.

Chapter Nine

Principles of Exposure Therapy

1) Understand your fear and subsequent reaction to it

By understanding that fear is a natural fraction of any confrontational situation and that your bodily reactions to it, like the adrenal reaction, are completely natural, you will be better prepared.

When I learned that everyone felt fear and that adrenalin was the friend of exceptional people, confronting my fears became a much easier task. Understanding that I hadn't failed because I still felt fear and that I and everyone else feels fear when confronting new situations helped me immeasurably.

I always thought that my goal should be to become fearless (it isn't) so I understandably felt like a failure every time I felt scared. When I later realised that fear is a natural bodily reaction felt by everyone and that the goal was to learn control, it acted as a calming balm. It's very hard to get somewhere, no matter how hard you try, when you have the wrong map. It was also soothing to realise that by trying I had already been successful; it was only when I didn't try that I failed.

2) Enter the fear syndrome

A scared young boxer named Cassius Clay (Mohammed Ali) fearfully approached his first entry to a boxing ring. A wise old boxing trainer, seeing that Clay was scared to enter the ring, said to the young fighter, 'Son, you should always confront those things that you fear.'

Plan ahead: don't enter blind. Imagine the good, the bad and the ugly. Mentally rehearse and visualise how you are going to react in all cases. See yourself handling setbacks positively; see yourself regaling in victory. Also imagine the consequences of success and the good and bad things that it might bring. See yourself handling these too. I always pictured myself the victor and used this as inspiration. I also looked at the worst-case scenario and visualised myself handling that gracefully.

I remember wanting to start training at a boxing club because I knew the exposure to good pugilists would help me with my own training in karate. However, I was worried that if I joined I might get knocked out. The pain element didn't worry me, it was more the embarrassment if it should happen. I knew that nothing of any worth ever came without risk so I visualised myself as an excellent boxer, which inspired me. I also watched a lot of boxing tapes and talked to boxers to gain yet more inspiration. Then I considered the worst-case scenario and told myself that if I got knocked out, I could handle it. Two years later I became an ABA boxing coach. I know many people who want the same qualification but cannot get over the cavernous risk hole.

As with my doing the boxing and using friends for support and inspiration, don't worry about enlisting the help of others, use them as a crutch. You may be surprised at the help you will get if only you ask. Eventually, as your confidence grows, you can discard the crutch (something that needs to be done at some stage) and continue unaided. Again, avoid those who might feed you with negative instead of positive data.

One of my friends told me I was 'mad' going to a boxing club. 'You'll end up with brain damage.' Then almost as an afterthought he said, 'but, if it's what you want to do…' Ye. Thanks for the encouragement. Others said, 'What do you want to do that for? Aren't you happy with what you've got?' as though my ambition was a greedy and selfish indulgence. Along the way you will quickly learn who to speak to and who to ignore.

Neil Adams, world champion Olympic silver medal judo player and reputedly the best judo player ever outside of Japan, is a great example of someone who embraced the fear syndrome to expand. Neil was winning just about everything there was to win in judo and it was obvious to all that he had major potential. However, he was rapidly becoming a huge fish in a small pond and was having to travel ever further afield to find competition. No one local was testing him and he had far outrun his present teachers. It was getting to the stage where he was teaching them as opposed to them teaching him. At this point many would have sat back on their laurels and remained on the plateau that they had reached. They never really improve from that point on. Neil realised this and at a very young age and moved away from his parents to live in London, thus enabling him to train full-time at the kodakan under the tuition of some of the world's finest judo-ka.

He made many sacrifices to get there, not least having to become a small fish in a big pond, but he felt the risk was worth it to get where he wanted to be. From reading Neil's autobiography it is obvious that he had to go through a lot of adversity in this tough club, but in the end he shone through. If it wasn't for his decision to move to London and train with the best, it is very doubtful that he would have reached the level he did.

id of your bodily reactions to confrontation

hat we have nothing to fear in life but fear is a lot closer to the truth than people might imagine. Anticipation is certainly more uncomfortable than confrontation. People often become so wrapped up in their fears that, in the end, they become more scared of the feelings that accompany confrontation than they do of the object of their fear. When you overanticipate, it opens the door to Mr Negative who, spotting your weakness, goes to work engineering the weakness until it becomes a gaping hole that he can walk right through. Once he gets through in mass you are sure to lose, probably before you even get close to the confrontation. As with the wrestler coming from Glasgow to fight Bert Asarati in London, you too will lose the fight at Birmingham. This will only happen if you become afraid of the feelings that are associated with confrontation, so don't be afraid of them.

'Easy to say!' I hear you cry. Listen, I've been there thousands of times and know the feeling well. That's all they are: feelings. They can't hurt you on their own. It is only your own panic that helps the feelings to burgeon. If you don't panic and tell yourself that you can handle it, they will eventually dissipate.

No one feeling can last forever,
Remember this when you endeavour
To conquer fear, and when depression creeps
In your mind this knowledge you should always keep.

This is a little poem that I used as a mantra whenever I was in a tricky situation and things started to feel ugly. No one feeling can last forever, it's true. Remember it and when things feel ugly for you, remind yourself, 'It can't last forever'. Also remind yourself that the feelings, however unnatural they may seem, are natural feelings that everyone feels at some time and they will only take control if you let them, so don't. It's your mind, it's your body; you're in charge and nobody else.

The more you are able to stay in the exposed situation the more you will realise that all I've stated is true. The more you become desensitised to the feelings of adrenalin, the stronger you will develop your mental muscle. No exposure, no expansion. Lots of exposure, lots of expansion. Be positive: control the inner opponent and there will be nothing that you will not be capable of.

4) Be active

I've always said, and we all know, that there are those that dream and there are those that do. I've been both in my time so can categorically say that dreaming as a single entity is about as useful as sugar wellingtons in a rainstorm. If you do nothing but dream you will achieve nothing. It is those that act who make those dreams reality.

Dreaming is very good if you marry it with action; it can act as a great stimulus and be very inspirational, and inspiration is rocket fuel that will enable you to reach the stars. Dreaming is a form of visualisation, a great way of seeing where you want to go, who you want to be, what you want to do. But, as I keep reiterating, if you want to learn to swim you have to get wet. So keep active, and do something every day, whether a lot or a little, to get where you want to be. Never put off until tomorrow: for dreamers, tomorrow never comes.

Draw out your road map, set your sights on realistic goals and go for it.

Think of your journey like a 120 mile walk from Birmingham to London. If you try to do it all in one go you are setting yourself up for disappointment. Be realistic, set yourself an achievable distance to do every day. If you think that you are comfortable with eight miles a day, stretch yourself and go for ten miles a day. In twelve days you will have achieved your goal, whereas if you had attempted the whole 120 miles in one or perhaps two goes you may well have taken on too much and become disheartened, eventually aborting the journey like so many people do.

I had a friend who wanted to get out of a bad relationship but was too afraid to leave. Just upping and going was something that he felt incapable of doing. He'd got to the stage where he was very miserable in his marriage but felt that there was no life for him outside it. His self-esteem was very low.

Rather than jumping in the deep end and just leaving his wife, he prepared himself very gradually by spending more and more time out of the marital home. It wasn't easy, his wife didn't like it and he had to fight every step of the way.

Whilst he was away from the house he took on a job that allowed him to socialise. He started to make many friends and this helped him to rebuild his broken confidence. He had also been afraid that if he left he might be homeless, but having checked up on the rental market he realised how simple getting a place of his own could be. Some of his new friends also offered him a room should he ever need it. Right towards the end of his marriage he even started going on overnight trips with some of his friends. Very soon he was spending more time out of the marital home than he was in it. When he eventually found the courage to leave it was not such a shock; after all, he'd spent the past six months preparing and practising. He also came to realise that most of the things that he was afraid might happen were very unlikely to, and if they did, he told himself, he would handle it.

5) Practice makes perfect

Although I might be stating the obvious here, practise is the only way of growing. If you practise you will get stronger; if you don't you won't.

No one ever got rich by just looking at the stock market, no one ever got a beach physique by just staring at the weights, no one ever became a world class martial artist without getting out there and practising and no one ever got successful by just lying in bed and dreaming about it.

Whilst it is true that the more you practise the quicker you will improve, it is also true that if you don't practise regularly enough your improvement will be very slow and there is more chance of you aborting the journey. So try to do something every day. If you leave too long between training sessions it is likely that the body will forget what it has learned and you will end up back at square one again. Use the inspiration of even the smallest success to fuel your next step by getting back to it as soon as possible; if you leave too long between practice sessions the inspirational fuel may be lost.

This is especially true with phobics. Even one step forward is better than staying stationary or moving backwards, and every single step counts. Taken on its own, one step may seem insignificant, but added to all the other steps taken over the period of one year, it is quite a distance. So practise, practise, practise and don't worry that it is hard; if it was easy everyone would be fearless and hugely successful.

6) Be realistic and fair to yourself

Being realistic is knowing your own limitations. Try not to bite off more than you can chew. If you do take on too much and suffer a setback, be fair to yourself. So many of my friends beat themselves up over silly setbacks. The fact that you are out there trying means that you are already a success. There will be many stumbles, even falls, on the road to a powerful self, so you have to prepare for them. Success is not never falling down, it is in always rising after falling. If you get knocked down seven times you must get up eight.

I don't know anyone who did not stumble or fall at one time or another. A stumble or fall is just another learning experience and the lessons learned cannot be learned in any other way. Recovering from a stumble or a fall and learning never to give in develops real character. True character is never really tested until you hit the deck. Like the boxers, it is not just about how big a punch you can throw, it's about how big a punch you can take. Whilst we endeavour not to stumble or fall, we also prepare ourselves for its eventuality, just in case. How do we prepare? By telling ourselves over and over again that, whatever happens, we can handle it.

If it does happen, pick yourself up, tend to your wounds and start again. Don't add insult to injury by letting your inner opponent tell you how bad it was of you to fall, how silly you looked when you fell, how ashamed you should be for falling, how you'll never recover from the fall, how everyone must be laughing at you falling and *Hey, I told you you couldn't do it, I knew you'd fall. Who the hell do you think you are for even trying?*

If you allow the inner opponent a podium he will make you feel ashamed for trying when really you should feel proud; he will make you feel pretentious when you should feel confident and ambitious, and he will make you feel weak when you should feel strong.

In brief, the inner opponent will make you feel completely worthless and will use any stumble or fall to underline and substantiate his negativity.

A Pat on the Back

It is also easy to become negative about those times when you do succeed. It is very important to remind yourself of how well you are doing. I would often feel very disillusioned if I was not gaining as quickly as I would have liked, my inner opponent telling me what a failure I was.

I remember climbing my pyramid of fears and struggling to get past a particular step. I was starting to feel strong and confident because I had managed to defeat fears on the lower steps of the pyramid, things that had hung over me for years. As soon as I stumbled on a particularly difficult fear my inner opponent was straight in there: *So, you thought you were strong. Not so strong now, are you? You're not strong at all, you're weak.*

Straight away I reminded myself that I was not weak, hadn't I already overcome some of my long standing fears at the bottom of the pyramid? My inner opponent, Mr Negative, was quick to maliciously point out that anyone could have overcome them. They were just kids' stuff. *Get to something half hard and what do you do? You fold like a piece of paper. That's all you are, a paperweight.*

Again, and at the risk of overemphasising the point, if you are out there trying then you are already a success and are already strong, any step forward is just that, a step forward. It should not be undermined, and should always be congratulated. All past victories should be used to emphasise and underline the fact that you are getting stronger. Whenever you struggle with a new challenge, use your past victories to reap strength. I used to drag up past victories to gain inspiration and to use as yardsticks many times when facing adversity. When I had a particularly nasty gang after me I drew strength from the fact that it wasn't the first time I'd had people after me and 'hey, if I handled it last time then I could handle it just as well this time.'

Success is not how you feel but how far you have gone

Very often people judge success by how they feel as opposed to how far they have gone. This is not the right way to look at it because as we approach a new situation and as we expand to take on new challenges we will feel fear. More than once I remember thinking 'I can't be getting any better, I still feel scared', totally forgetting the early lessons that *fear will never go away as long as I continue to grow,* and *everyone feels fear when confronting new situations.* I had to remind myself not only of these lessons but also of the fact that many of the things that I had feared all my life I had left decimated in my wake and that

I was now doing and achieving things that I never dreamed possible. Even though I was not yet at the top of my fear pyramid I was already living a brave and exciting life and for the first time since I was a child I no longer felt at the mercy of my inner opponent.

It's a little like going on a hundred-mile journey in your car. If the car breaks down after eighty miles it doesn't mean that the journey is over and it doesn't mean that once you have fixed the car you have to start again. No matter what happens you have still successfully travelled eighty miles and you still have only twenty miles to go. OK, your success has been slowed a little, but you can handle that. Take a positive attitude to your hurdles and pitfalls. If my car breaks down because I didn't put enough water in the engine before setting out then I'll learn from that, next time I set off on a long journey I'll make sure I top up the water first. Remember, it's not how you feel it's how far you have gone.

7) Use a helper

Don't be afraid of using a helper, preferably someone who has trodden the same path and come through. Read books and listen to inspirational tapes. Inspiration is the fuel that will get you where you want to be, but it will need topping up regularly. When you feel inspired, act.

There is no better person to talk to than someone who is where you want to be; they will make you feel like you can walk on water. Even being around successful people will make you feel good and make you feel like you can achieve, confront, change, grow, succeed. If your will is a little low and no one is to hand, use the phone, write a letter, watch a video, listen to a tape. Just the fact that you are doing these things is an excellent sign because it means you are taking action and you are fighting and beating the inner opponent. No matter how bad you feel, just do it. I guarantee you'll feel better afterwards. Every time you beat the inner opponent you will be developing a little more mental muscle. Making decisions and taking action means that you are taking control and control of the self is what makes success.

You don't have to do everything alone, even now I'll phone people if I need a little inspiration, or I'll read a book or listen to a tape. A good friend will allow you to let off steam when things aren't going quite to plan and they'll let you talk about plans and reap inspiration when things are good. If your batteries are a little low use a crutch to kick-start you back into action.

Also, a helper who has trodden the same path will invariably have had to overcome the same hurdles. So when you say, 'You'll never guess what happened to me today', they'll invariably say, 'Oh yeah, I remember when that happened to me. This is what I did to get past it.'

Knowing that someone else has gone through the same problems and overcome them will bring great solace. There is nothing worse than thinking that you are the only person in the world who is feeling or experiencing what you're feeling or experiencing. I remember ringing up my helper for advice on a particularly trying problem, feeling all the worse because I thought the problem unique to me. 'Oh, you don't want to worry about that,' he told me convincingly. 'Exactly the same thing happened to me, it happens to nearly everyone.' I can't tell you the relief that I felt knowing that it wasn't just me and that the problem I was facing was a common one.

Where I used people as helpers then, I act as a helper to others now, as will you. And when they speak to you fearfully about the things they are experiencing you will laugh to yourself and find it hard to believe that you too once felt the same way. With hind-sight your old fears will seem as silly as your new life will feel exciting.

Whilst it is not a nice thing, you should also take strength from those around you who fall. I'm not saying that you shouldn't help those that might be struggling, of course you should, but there will be those you cannot help for whatever reason. Use their failure to give you strength.

On the one or two occasions on the door when my fellow doormen lost their bottle in the midst of a bad situation and left their post, I would unashamedly reap strength from their lack. This is not a selfish thing, far from it, panic and submission has a habit of being infectious. If people around you are losing it, it is very easy for their weakness to drag you down too, so you have to go straight to the offensive and think, 'They're losing it and I'm still here, that means I'm strong. I'm not going to fall like them. I'm going to stick with it.'

You'll be surprised at how you can make this work for you. I've watched people who I'd previously thought were very strong, falling by the wayside whilst I continued on. I remember thinking, 'I thought they were really strong people and look at me; I'm stronger than they are. And I'm going to get even stronger'. So, good or bad, use it.

8) Group support

This is not something that I have used personally but I still think that it is an excellent idea to surround yourself with people of the same ilk as yourself. You will be able to reap advice and enthusiasm from those above you and offer help to those below. The learning experience from group therapy is tremendous and the benefits unparalleled. Everything needed to help you overcome your fears will be in the one room – surely an inspirational experience.

9) Admit your fears to others

Whilst this isn't imperative, it may be helpful. It is hard to enlist the help of others if they don't know how you're feeling. In the early days my greatest helper was my mother. Of course as a young person I felt ashamed to admit to her how I was feeling in case she thought me weak, but, as she always told me, 'I can't help you if I don't know what it is you're worried about'. Some of the things that I was scared of made me feel ashamed and I was convinced that if I told anyone I would be a laughing stock and that my mum would rush me straight down the doctor's. To my absolute amazement it turned out that my fears were quite natural and manageable. If I didn't admit those early fears to my mum I'd probably still be dealing with them to this day.

One of my friends was having terrible fights with his wife. She couldn't understand why he wouldn't take the wonderful new job that he'd been offered that he'd been working towards for a long time and that promised them the lifestyle they had always dreamed of.

He wanted the job but was afraid to take it in case he couldn't handle the pressure of change and it didn't work out. The job he had wasn't good but it was safe. He worried that if he didn't like the new job he might be tied to it by the subsequent lifestyle that came with it and by the higher mortgage payments that came with the new home that the higher salary would enable them to buy.

His worst fear was that if everything went wrong he might lose his wife, and they were already arguing (his inner opponent constantly reminded him of this fact). In his frightened state he even wondered whether the arguing and rows were omens that the job change was not right. He daren't tell his wife of his fears because she had always seen him as a strong man and he didn't want her to think otherwise. So, rather than tell her of his fears outright he made up excuses as to why he didn't want to take on the new job, excuses that his wife could not come to terms with.

When things finally came to a head and he did tell her of his fears he was astounded at her sympathetic and supportive response. What she made him realise was that he was not alone; whatever the outcome was, good or bad, they would share it and they would always be together. With the help of his wife my friend took on the new job and with it a new and better life-style. The fact that he had confided in his wife also brought them closer together. If he hadn't shared his fears, who knows what might have happened?

10) Finish what you have started

Once you have started to climb the fear pyramid, it is important to finish. It is very easy to attain a measure of success and then stop growing. If you want complete control you need a complete victory, if you only climb half or three quarters of the way up the pyramid then you are only partially in control. The problem with partial control is that it often lapses back to no control. It's a little like only taking half a course of antibiotics; you feel a lot better so you don't finish the prescribed course and the next thing you know you're ill again because the infection wasn't completely cured. Similarly when treating a cancer it is imperative that the whole tumour is removed or the patient will certainly regress as the tumour inevitably grows back to full strength.

Often people get close to the top of the pyramid and then stop, saying, 'Well, I feel a lot better now, I'm happy with the fact that I've got this far. I don't need to confront that last fear, I think I've done enough already.'

Usually this is just an excuse that the inner opponent invents, one of many, to stop growth. So if you want complete control, complete the course.

Chapter Ten

The Fear Pyramid

'I believe that anyone can conquer fear by doing the things he fears to do, provided he keeps doing them until he gets a record of successful experiences behind him.'

Eleanor Roosevelt

The method that I employed to generate and ultimately control fear was the fear pyramid. This can often be a very private thing. A lot of people will not wish to share their more private fears with others and this reticence is understandable, though it is hard to enlist the help of others if you do not tell them what it is you fear. It is imperative, though, that you do admit them, even if it is only to yourself; don't fob yourself off as I once did with feeble excuses like, 'I'm not scared of it [whatever 'it' may be], I just don't want to do it', and other such inanities.

That is the first and most important step, you can go no further until it is complete. These are the three preparatory steps:

1) Make a list of all your fears.

2) Draw yourself a pyramid with as many steps up to the pinnacle as you have fears.

3) Fill each of those steps with one of your listed fears, starting at the bottom of the pyramid with your least fear and finishing at the top step with your greatest fear.

The common factor with all fears is that confronting them will cause an adrenal rush. It is anticipation that sparks adrenalin, as opposed to the actual fear itself.

FRED'S FEAR PYRAMID

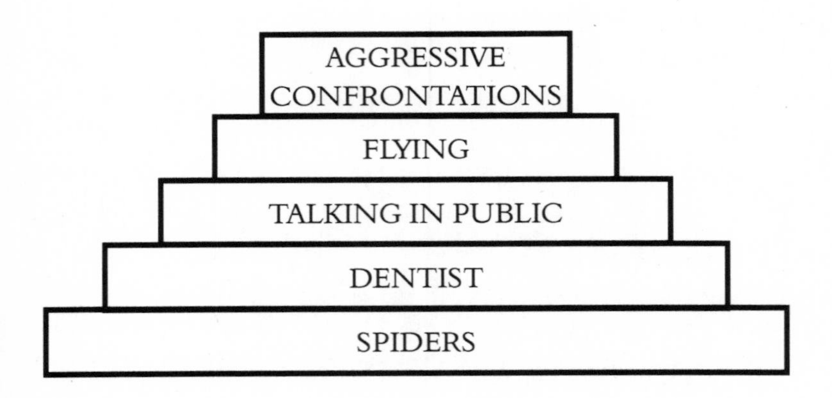

This is a hypothetical example, I've no doubt that your pyramid will be filled with completely different fears to Fred's.

Fred has filled his pyramid with all his own fears. He is scared of spiders, but of all his fears this one is his least. We do not want to try and run before we can walk, so we will get Fred to confront this one first, by finding a spider and picking it up, using the aforementioned A, R and O theory of fear control.

Accept the fear, recognise that it is adrenalin and a natural feeling, then override the feeling and pick up the spider. Fred has to accept that he has a fear of the spider, recognise the feeling of adrenalin, counter any negative thoughts with positive ones and then override the feeling by picking up the spider.

It will not be easy to start with so don't expect it to be, you may well spend half an hour in anticipation during which time you may feel all of the aforementioned bodily reactions to adrenalin; it may even take you weeks or months to summon up the courage. The decision to try is your first victory. By making the decision you have taken control and won your first fight with the inner opponent.

Once Fred has managed to pick up the spider he should put it down and do it again and again until he no longer holds the fear. Once the fear is erased Fred should then progress to the second step on the pyramid and his second least fear, then repeat the process all the way up the pyramid until he reaches the peak.

All of the aforementioned techniques and knowledge should be used in the execution of confrontation.

Sometimes one confrontation may be enough to deem you completely desensitised to the fear, other times you may have to repeat the confrontation several times. Fred may have to pick the spider up six times before he completely loses his fear of spiders, and yet only one visit to the dentist may see his fear of dentists decimated.

The speed with which you travel through your pyramid of fears depends entirely upon yourself. It took me several years to get to the top of mine, though the overall time matters not, as long as you are working on a day to day basis. As I said before, if you leave too long between practice sessions the fuel of inspiration may be lost and the subconscious mind may forget the lessons learned from your last victory.

With every fear you erase you will be gaining some degree, large or small, of mental strength, desensitisation and exposure to adrenalin and self-discipline. Every step you climb up the pyramid will make you increasingly stronger and give you more control over the inner opponent.

To many, the fears at the bottom of your pyramid such as picking up a spider or visiting the dentist may seem an eternity away from confronting and controlling the fears at the top of your pyramid. I agree that they do seem poles apart but they are directly related because both scenarios require self-discipline and fear control, albeit in varying degrees.

The importance of the smaller fears is that they actually build self-discipline and help to develop a control over fear, which are pivotal in the extension of the 'cut out' point. Also, by confronting minor fears you are getting regular exposure to adrenalin. In theory, picking up a spider when you hold a fear of it, is the same as controlling the fear so evident in a confrontational situation with an assailant. Granted, they are at different ends of the 'fear' scale, but that is all that differentiates them.

As you go further up the pyramid, that gap decreases more and more with every step. For instance, on Fred's pyramid, his fear of flying and confrontational situations are separated by one step, and once he has confronted and erased his fear of sparring there is no longer a gap at all.

Getting Past Sticking Points – The Inner Pyramid

It is inevitable that at some stage you may reach a sticking point and no matter what you do or how hard you try you just cannot physically get past it. Whenever I reached a sticking point and I found a fear too great to confront outright I would use an inner pyramid, which allowed me to break the fear down into smaller, more manageable components, like the 100-mile journey we spoke of earlier in the book. Rather than try to travel the whole hundred miles in one go, you can break the journey down into ten sections of ten miles, or even twenty sections of five miles. We can do the same here using the inner pyramid.

For example, if you had a fear of spiders and could not break the fear in one fell swoop by simply picking one up, the inner pyramid would look something like this:

INNER PYRAMID

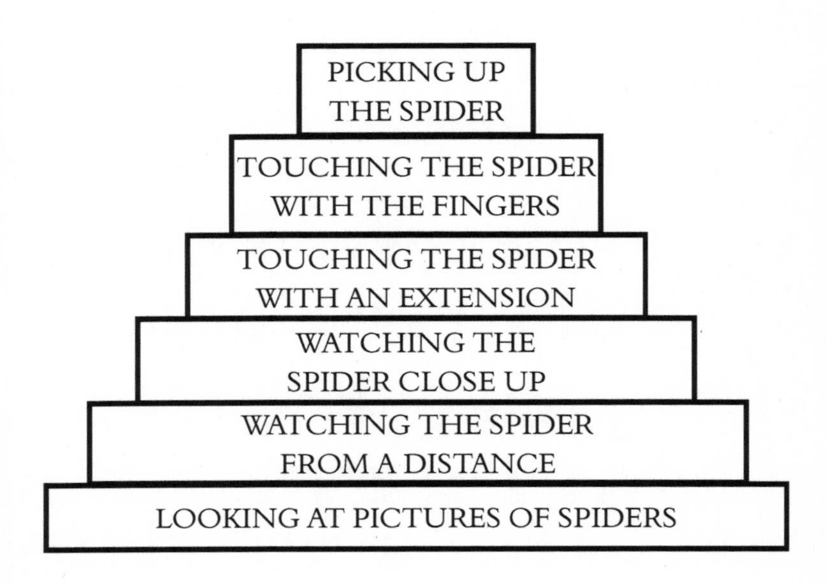

As you can see, the inner pyramid allows you to approach your fear in small stages, each stage allowing you to build confidence and gain desensitisation to the fear. En route you will defeat your inner opponent by confronting each section when he tells you that you should or could not. You should also use a helper to gain inspiration and read books to get a better understanding of spiders and to prove to your doubting mind that spiders cannot harm you (there is little point in picking up a deadly spider, nearly everyone would be afraid of such a task and rightfully so).

Look at the worst-case scenario and accept that, if the worst should happen, you'd handle it. You should systematically confront one step at a time, being sure not to leave each step until you are completely comfortable with it. Before you know it you will be holding the spider in your hand without any fear. Then you will be ready to move on to the next step and the next fear.

As another example, this is how I broke down my fear of joining a boxing club into more manageable sections.

INNER PYRAMID

I talked to people who knew about boxing and drew inspiration from them. They also told me about the workings of a modern

Western boxing gym and what I should expect when I joined. I watched as much boxing as I could to desensitise myself to the rigours of contact and to gain an understanding of their strategies. I also copied what I saw in the videos on the punch bag in my garage. I went to watch a boxing class in action, again to aid desensitisation.

It's hard to see clearly what the mind has got completely out of focus. Your subconscious mind has a way of making things seem twice as big and scary as they really are; allowing the conscious mind to see the 'real deal' gets rid of any myths that the sub-conscious mind may have manufactured. Eventually I actually went to the boxing club to train. It was nowhere near as bad as I had envisaged, but then few things are.

As for the fear of humiliation, I just told myself that no matter what happened I could handle it, it was worth the risk. It's like the friend I spoke of earlier in the book who wanted to get out of a bad, long-term relationship, but felt that the world outside of that relationship would be too hostile and unforgiving. To rid himself of the myth he went out and had a good look at what he was letting himself in for. Far from being hostile and unforgiving he found many new friends and experienced happiness for the first time in years.

One of my friends, Jim Brown, is a British champion skydiver. He knows that every time he jumps out of the plane he risks death, but to him the pleasure that he gets from skydiving is worth the ultimate risk.

Others feel that taking a business gamble is worth the risk of losing money or even losing everything. Whatever the risk, if you really want something you have to be prepared to handle it.

Rising Self-esteem

Running parallel with the fear pyramid is your level of rising self-esteem. With every fear that you confront and beat, your self-esteem will rise and your confidence will grow. You will be better able to handle the things that life throws at you and subsequently be happier without the constant barrage of worries under the dominion of which most people live. At the bottom of the scale you are in a position of weakness: at the top of the scale, a position of power.

On the way up the pyramid you will often have to overcome hurdles and pitfalls and the road may sometimes be rocky. When you are faced with hurdles and pitfalls, overcome them; when you are not, don't throw rocks in your own way. I would often reach a high and think, 'This is going far too easily. When is the bubble going to burst?' My inner opponent would manufacture problems to halt my progress. If you are going through a good patch, enjoy it; when you're going through a bad patch, handle it.

Rewards

A great incentive for improvement is to give yourself rewards for goals achieved. If you are working on the fear pyramid, give yourself a reward for every successful step that you take. Even if you are working on the inner pyramid you could give yourself a reward for every two steps successfully taken. This will really give you something to go for. Confronting the fear is a reward in itself but because it is intangible it is often difficult to appreciate, so tangible rewards are good incentives.

Going out for a nice meal, or a night at a show, even having a day off practice might be a good incentive (as long as a day doesn't become a week). Whenever I overcame a difficult task I would make a picnic for me and my lady and go to a local nature park for the morning and really chill out. It might even be an idea to pyramid the rewards with the fears: as you confront bigger fears, give yourself bigger rewards. When enthusiasm is low it is often the thought of a nice reward that pulls you through.

Handling Distress

Working on the premise that the fear never goes away, and due to the fact that you are constantly confronting new fears, the only way to judge your progress is to see how far you have gone as opposed to how you feel. Having said that, with each successive, successful confrontation you will become more and more desensitised to the feelings associated with confrontation. Whilst you are getting stronger and stronger you will still feel the effects of adrenalin, or fight or flight.

The way of handling the distress caused by the constant exposure to your fear is to remember that the feelings will not last forever, they are completely natural and feelings cannot in themselves hurt you. Some people even learn to like the feeling and look for it to give them a buzz. These people are called adrenalin junkies.

If the feeling is becoming stressful, remind yourself of these things and tell yourself again that no matter how bad it gets, you can handle it. To reassure yourself, think back to other times when you felt adrenalin. Probably the worst thing that happened was that you felt uncomfortable to the degree that you wanted to get away from the situation that was causing adrenal release.

Being a self-defence instructor I often come across people who tell me that they feel like cowards because they had previously run away from a potentially violent situation. One told me, 'I've been training for twenty years and yet when the fight kicked off I just ran away. I felt so scared. I feel like such a coward.'

He wasn't a coward; he just misread the signs. What his reasoning process saw as fear was really adrenalin and he completely misread his own bodily reactions to conflict.

A friend who was scared of moving to a better job told me, 'I've been working all my life for this opportunity and when it's finally offered to me on a plate I haven't got the guts to go for it.' He felt like a coward and as if he was letting everyone down. He too misread the signs. The feelings he was experiencing were all natural.

Knowledge dispels fear.

Chapter Eleven

Visualisation

'Seeing is achieving! Whatever the mind of man can conceive he can achieve.'

Samuel Johnson

'It's been said that imagination is stronger than will-power and by not trying, by just visualising the goal accomplished it can be easier to achieve in real life.'

Takayuki Kubota

Top golfers are unanimous in their praise for it, champion bodybuilders put it on a par with diet, and doctors and psychologists universally use it with great success, yet it still lies largely in the shadow of disbelief and ignorance. Some sceptics may laugh at the very thought of programming your mind, via visualisation, but who can argue with documented fact (or Tak Kubota for that matter)? I think that visualisation is best summed up by the psychologists Samuels and Samuels: 'What people visualise is what they get, likewise, what they have is a result of what they have visualised.'

Visualisation is a many splendoured thing in that it can be used to attain many things, from building up confidence to perfecting technique and confronting fears. In a documented experiment in America (one of many putting visualisation to the test), two groups of students were given the task of practising basketball penalty shots every day for a month.

One group actually physically practised netting the ball whilst the other group lay on a bed or sat in a chair and, using visualisation, mentally practised netting the ball. At the end of the month both groups met up at a basketball court and physically competed to see which of the two could net the most shots. The group that had practised using visualisation won by a considerable margin.

You shouldn't *replace* physical practice with visualisation, but certainly use it as a strong supplement. I have successfully commissioned the use of visualisation on many occasions, and genuinely believe that almost anything is attainable through its conscientious practice.

'All we have is a result of what we have thought.'

Dhamnapada (psychologist)

Many top martial arts competitors are starting to latch on to visualisation and the benefits it can offer. Chuck Norris, in his competition days, used it before he fought and said that many times he scored points on his opponents with the exact moves he had beaten them with in his mind's eye only minutes before.

Floro Villabrille, the famous unbeaten Filipino martial artist who was the victor of countless full contact escrima and kali matches practised visualisation whilst he actually trained. He would always go up to the mountains, alone, before a match and in his imagination would fight his opponent over and over again until he felt he couldn't lose. He was quoted as saying, 'I can't lose, when I enter the ring nobody can beat me; I already know that man is beaten.'

Before I describe the methods of visualisation, let's first examine what the famous humanistic psychologist, Abraham Maslow, termed the Jonah Complex, or in layman's terms, the fear of success.

In the bible, Jonah was told by God to save the people of the city of Ninevah from their sinfulness. Afraid of failing, he ran away to sea, only for the ship to be hit by a severe storm. To appease God, the crew threw Jonah into the sea where he was swallowed by a whale. Jonah prayed to God, who saved him. Jonah went to Ninevah and preached to the people who repented and were saved by God. Maslow believed that we are all a little bit like Jonah: too scared to fulfill our greatest potential. You maybe surprised to learn that the Jonah Complex stifles the advancement of as many people as the fear of failure.

Maslow stated that,

'We are generally afraid to become that which we can glimpse in our most perfect moments; under the most perfect conditions, under conditions of greatest courage we enjoy and even thrill to the godlike possibilities we see in ourselves at such peak moments, and yet simultaneously shiver with weakness, awe and fear before the same possibilities.'

Many people in the martial arts would, for instance, enjoy the prestige of representing their national squad, but how many of those same people, I wonder, would relish the thought of facing top-flight competitors at squad meetings once a month? Not so many I think!

Methods of Practice

Visual rehearsal, self-actualisation, going to the movies or visualisation; call it what you will, the process is basically the same and really quite a simple way of utilising a little more of your mental muscle.

Initially, the best way of practising visualisation is lying down in a quiet, darkened room. Close your eyes, breathe in and out deeply and relax. Once a relaxed state is acquired try to picture in your mind's eye your desired goal. At first you might find this difficult, but with practice it will get easier and the mental images clearer.

Picture yourself facing your fears or utilising your game plan in a confrontation again and again, until it is well and truly programmed into your mind. Try to see the desired goal in as much detail as possible. The brain finds it very difficult to discern between what is imagined and what is actual, all it knows is what is programmed into it, so when you come to perform the goal that you've visualised, the brain gets straight into gear; you've rehearsed it so often it thinks it has done it before.

Many people who already practise visualisation only use one of the senses – sight – out of the possible five (sight, smell, hearing, touch and taste). Psychologists talk of the three out of five rule. Using three out of your five senses, they say, will enhance your visualisation practice. Tom Platze, 'Mr Legs', one of the world's greatest bodybuilders said, 'If you can use five of your senses in visualisation practice I'm confident that you can triple the results of your visualisation process.'

Here is an example. If your goal is to employ your chosen game plan in a confrontation with a bully, then utilise the three out of five rule. Imagine the 'feel' of fear within you and confidently controlling that fear. Try to see and hear your bully before you, and hear your voice refusing to baulk to his threats. Perhaps as a climax see, hear and feel yourself verbally standing up for yourself and the bully backing down.

The more real and the more detailed you make your imagined performance the better your results will be.

I often practised visualisation just before I went out to work as a doorman in the nightclubs. I mentally rehearsed techniques that have been successful for me in the past (it's always easier to visualise something that you have experienced before). In this sense I have found its practice an invaluable asset.

Going to the Movies

As a final note, if you have trouble visualising images try 'going to the movies'. In your mind's eye imagine a huge cinema screen in front of you, with yourself on the screen succeeding in your desired goal. Make the image as vivid as possible, use the three out of five rule, repeat the sequence as often as you can (fifteen minutes a day) and it will eventually become programmed into your mind. But please remember it is not a substitute, but an addition to physical training.

Chapter Twelve

Dealing with Killjoys

You know, one of my greatest realisations and disappointments with succeeding and growing was when others would not grow with me or reacted badly to my success.

When I started to experience a degree of success with my writing and had appeared on the television a couple of times, many of the people around me began to change for the worse.

A very close friend became abrupt and overcritical, even down-right rude, telling me that no one liked my books and that I should keep my feet on the ground. Another told me emphatically that my first book had nothing but a novelty factor and would never sell outside of my local city. He felt it was his absolute duty to tell me this as if to say, 'Who the hell do you think you are trying to become a writer?'

Another associate scoffed when I told him, a little shyly, that I wanted to become a full-time writer. He let me know in not so many words that I'd done OK (with added emphasis on *OK*) to get one book published but 'don't start getting above your station'. People I hardly knew told my friends, 'Oh yeah, Geoff Thompson, you can't speak to him now that he's made it. Who does he think he is?'

When I told people of my ambitions they told me I was a dreamer; when I succeeded I suddenly became a big-head. I can't tell you how disappointed I was with this attitude. For a while there I let them hold me back, thinking that maybe they were right. If people tell you often enough that you won't make it (and you listen to them) you start to believe it. They say that you find out who your friends are when you hit the bottom but it is also true that you find out who they are when you reach the top as well.

There can be many reasons for this negativity and understanding them can help you to cope with and even help the killjoys.

Envy

Friends often feel envious because you have reached a place that they would love to be.

Fear

Close friends and relatives often fear that your success will leave them out in the cold, that you will no longer want them if you 'make it'. They show their fear by trying to hold you back in any way they can.

Insecurity

The reason why lots of people do not or will not grow is because they feel secure in their comfort zones. Part of that security comes from the fact that most of their friends and relatives share the same zone, so when you expand and leave that zone, to their subconscious minds it is almost like you have deserted them.

Resentment

My growth out of the comfort zone caused a lot of resentment, especially from some friends and training companions who thought, in some cases *knew*, that they were as good as me, even though they did not have the bottle or foresight to do anything with their talent. They put my success down to pure luck.

'You're lucky that you got a break,' one told me.

'Yeah, you're right,' I replied sarcastically. 'I was lucky. And you know the funny thing; the more I practise the luckier I seem to get.'

People will give you a million sob stories about how they could have made it if only they got a break. In this world you have to make your own breaks, even the bible tells us that God helps those who help themselves.

Disorientation

Another reason why people stay in safe zones is because they fear change; change causes disorientation. The sad thing is that if *you* change and you are an integral part of their comfort zone, this will cause them disorientation.

Anger

Your loved ones become angry. Why? Because you're strong now and whilst you still love them they know that you don't need them so much. Once they were your moral crutch, but now that you are mended you don't need a crutch. 'Oh you don't need me now. That wasn't the story last year; you were on the phone to me every day for support.' A little like a walking stick saying, 'Oh, that's right, throw me in the cupboard now that your broken leg is healed. Now that you don't need me, just throw me out with yesterday's rubbish.'

As silly as this may sound this is how many people feel. They fear not being needed, and like the walking stick they feel that they were used.

Part of practice is using crutches to help you expand, just as part of succeeding is letting go of the crutches so that you can complete the process. It is very easy to become attached to your crutch (for want of a better expression) and feel that you will never be able to walk without it. If you don't let go of it and try you will never be able to walk without it.

So the remedy is to explain to your friends and loved ones that you love them and need them as much as ever but their reticence to let you fly the nest is hampering your growth and causing you to resent them. But please, have patience with them. Often the people closest to us fear abandonment, and when they feel and fear this they really are in pain. Try to soothe them and let them know that whilst you are growing and moving in a new direction that doesn't mean that you don't want them to be a major part of that growth. Tell them that you want to take them with you.

I have to tell you that I have felt this fear myself and it is a very lonely and sad feeling. When you feel like this you just want people to tell you that they love and need you to be a part of their lives whichever way they go. So be patient, try to understand and help those around you as you help yourself.

Dave was almost at the stage of giving up on one of his friends because of their anger and resentment at Dave's growth and success. Every time that Dave went to see his mate he would make Dave feel guilty and depressed so in the end he started avoiding him. This of course added fuel to the fire, 'Dave never comes around to see me any more. Probably thinks that I'm not good enough for him now that he's doing well.' Dave didn't go around to see him any more because when he did he was made to feel bad.

As a last ditch attempt at keeping the friendship alive Dave rang up his mate and asked to meet him to have a talk about things. Dave confronted his friend about his bad attitude. At first his friend said that he didn't know what he was talking about but then said, 'Well, I'm your mate. I'm just trying to keep your feet on the floor and stop you from getting big-headed. Someone has to.'

Dave told him, 'Look, I'm forty years old, I don't need anyone to keep my feet on the floor and if my mates can't be a little more supportive with me then what kind of mates are they? Honestly, I'm getting to the stage where I don't want to be in your company any more because you make me feel so depressed.'

This came as a shock to Dave's mate who hadn't realised that his constant barrage of put-downs was losing him his best mate. Realising this and the fact that he wasn't going to lose Dave as a friend just because of a little success (this was probably the main thing that he was worried about), he made an about turn and he and Dave quickly became close again.

The moral of this true story is this: try your very best to understand those who are not growing with you and reassure them. Let them know that you still love them and need them and that you very much want them as an integral part of your life. Soothe their pain if you can. We have all been there so it is not hard to empathise with that. If you can't make them see, then you may find that you lose them from your life. They will probably tell everyone that it is entirely your fault, that you changed and that success went to your head. You see it in the papers every day with famous celebrities whose friends and ex-lovers are claiming that they were deserted as soon as the person became famous. This is part of success and should be dealt with, as usual, by telling yourself that you can handle it. But please try and help others before you let them go.

Chapter Thirteen

Hurdles and Pitfalls

'Nothing of any value ever came without a fight.'

'On the long journey from A to Z you learn an awful lot about B to Y.'

'There is often a lot more merit in what you learn on the journey than what you find at the journey's end.'

'If there is no adversity there is no advance.'

Geoff Thompson

No matter what it is you are trying to achieve in life, whether it is excellence in the martial arts, faster track times in the world of athletics, building up a successful business or even maintaining a healthy relationship with your partner, you are always going to have the hindrance of hurdles and pitfalls.

In your own mind the inner opponent, Mr Negative, can and will hinder your chances of success in any field, if not taken to task and controlled. The mind can be like an overbearing parent, frightened to give his child too much control. As soon as you start to gain a little competence and get a little way up the mountain of self-realisation, the mind throws something tangible or intangible in your way to slow you down or stop you completely.

The further you get up that mountain and the more hurdles you climb over and pitfalls you cross, the stronger you become and the more control you gain over your own mind. At the top of the mountain is the ultimate goal of complete self-control. On the journey you will have developed an iron will and an indomitable spirit through having overcome hurdles and pitfalls.

You will also gain enlightenment, because in order to get over some of the more difficult hurdles and pitfalls, it is necessary to dissect yourself mentally; admitting and recognising your weaknesses in order to be able to confront and overcome them, and thus get past whatever stumbling block it is that's holding you back. This mental dissection is what develops into enlightenment. This is why hurdles and pitfalls are, in essence, a godsend. Without the challenge they provide, you wouldn't find enlightenment, you wouldn't develop the iron will that is necessary to confront them nor the indomitable spirit that is developed by never giving in to them when the going gets tough.

Metaphorically it is a little like immersing an inner tube into a bowl of water and filling it with air to find out if there are any leaks. Once you have found the leaks you can patch them up. Ultimately, you will have no leaks.

You have to treat your whole journey like you were training for a marathon or for a black belt. If you see it as such it helps to keep things in perspective.

The hurdles and pitfalls are or can be many splendoured. They may be tangible or intangible. Sometimes when there are no hurdles imminent, the mind, wishing to abort the journey, will invent silly ones.

Basically speaking, hurdles and pitfalls come in three categories, though are uniform in one element: they are all reasons to give in, and are nearly always thrown in when the recipient is just starting to gain some kind of realisation and competence. Recognising them as hurdles and pitfalls and realising that the real benefits to be had from training are gained only by overcoming them will help immeasurably in your bid to do so.

The three categories of reasons not to continue the metaphoric journey are *Tangible*, *Intangible* and *Silly Reasons*.

Tangible Reasons

These are incidental hurdles and pitfalls that are responsible for more people throwing in the towel than any other reason. Broken bones, torn ligaments, twisted ankles, illnesses (one of my students once missed two months' training because, and I quote, 'Me mum's got to 'ave an 'isterectomy'); the list goes on. With a serious injury it is foolish not to rest up as the injury or illness may be aggravated by your continuance. However, minor injuries should not deter you from your goal. You can quite easily work around such injuries. I have had broken bones all over my body, but still managed to train. Continuing under such adverse conditions requires and develops real willpower and is a great character builder.

With the more serious injury or illness that does lay you off, the danger lies in whether or not you get back to your journey after your convalescence. From my experience, most people do not. While you are recovering, try to maintain your enthusiasm and ties with your goal, this will greatly help in your re-start program when the obstacle of bad health is removed. A lot of people use their injuries to opt out because they were finding the going getting tough anyway, but remember this: if it was easy everybody would be in receipt of their dreams. If there is no adversity there is no advance.

Intangible Reasons

These can be as destructive in your advancement as the tangibles, and in a psychological sense far more painful. Also, because they are mental as opposed to physical, they can quite often be very difficult to admit or detect. The greatest intangible in martial arts is physical contact: sparring or getting hit. A great percentage of people leave training because they are frightened of sparring. Even at the boxing club when I was coaching, it was common knowledge that you lost eighty-five per cent of your new starters after you put them in the ring for the first time.

The only way to overcome this fear is to confront it again and again until you become desensitised to it, and take heart; it does get better. The more you practise and put yourself in the firing line, the better and more confident you will feel.

Boredom

'It's getting boring.' If I had a penny for every time I've heard this excuse! Boredom is another major pitfall that loses many people from the martial arts arena and in my opinion, it is a lazy excuse. To develop a technique into an instinctive reflex, to develop power, speed, endurance, footwork or anything else worth having for that matter, requires repetition, and what is repetition if it isn't boring?

Repetition is practised by the student revising for his doctorate, and by the soldier perfecting a bayonet attack. Swimmers will practise for hours and hours a day perfecting a stroke and jugglers will juggle until their hands bleed: all in pursuit of excellence. Boredom is the lazy man's excuse not to practise. You must treat boredom as another challenge, hurdle or pitfall that must be overcome if advancement is to be attained. When boredom sets in you must use concentration to push it back out again. Sheer concentration on the technique you are practising will erode boredom.

Lack of Enjoyment

Lack of enjoyment in practice goes hand in hand with boredom. Another feeble excuse. Enjoyment in practice comes and goes; nobody enjoys it all of the time. The real enjoyment comes from the fruits of training rather than the actual training itself. After all, to become proficient we must push ourselves through the pain of a gruelling training session. Who in their right mind enjoys pain (my profuse apologies to all you masochists out there!)?

If you are going through a bad patch of not enjoying your training, stick with it and try to treat the training as a mundane task that has to be done. The enjoyment will return. It's unrealistic to expect enjoyment all the time out of something so physically and mentally demanding. When the enjoyment is there, make the best of it; when it isn't, cope. It's all part of the character-building process.

Lack of Improvement or Success

Another favourite excuse for throwing in the towel is, 'I don't seem to be getting any better.' This is one of the mind's best finishers and kills off many students with the suddenness of cyanide tea; after all, what is the point of continuing in training if you're not getting any better? If I may use a metaphor, it is like a propelling spiral that picks up momentum very quickly but just as it seems to be reaching its pinnacle of speed, it starts (or at least it would appear) to go backwards.

So it is with your journey. In the beginning you are learning something new every day and improvement can be as fast as the metaphoric spiral. All of a sudden your advancement seems to be slowing down and in some cases you seem (like the spiral) to be going backwards instead of forwards, but it is only an illusion. After such a quick advance even a slight decrease in speed may seem like a backward spiral but usually it is only the person himself who sees, or thinks they see, this supposed decline; every-one else around them will be seeing their improvement.

From my experience it is ironically usually the better student who thinks he isn't improving. Every day and every session that you train will bring you some advancement visible or invisible, large or small. The child that you see every day will show no visible change or growth but to the person who only sees the same child every few months, the change is so obvious that they sometimes can't believe it's the same child. And so it is with improvement in training: sometimes it is so gradual that on a day to day basis it is almost unnoticeable, but it will be there.

Silly Reasons

These are the most infuriating and are always employed by people who are using a silly excuse to cover a deeper, more underlying reason or problem. These are the worst (and sometimes the funniest) reasons for missing single sessions of training or even packing it in altogether, because it means that the person employing the silly excuse cannot come to terms with the real reason.

Here are my favourite silly reasons, all of which have been used to me by my own karate students over the years:

I can't practise or continue because...

My cat died (a great excuse because it can be used nine times)

My mother is having a hysterectomy (I think he was getting sympathy pains)

My karate suit is in the wash (as coincidence would have it, the Cup Final coincided with my training time and this was just one of the many excuses used that night)

I haven't got any money (saw him in the pub, drunk, later that night)

My granddad died (third time this year)

I had to go to a funeral (hope it's not his granddad again)

My wife's ill (my club is on Wednesdays and Sundays. Coincidentally these are the only days that she gets ill)

It was raining (he must be made of sugar)

My mum's varicose veins are playing her up (what?)

I can't take my grading because my flat's flooded and my daughter fell off her bike (the grading wasn't for another six weeks)

Obviously, some of these reasons can be genuine, but every reason not to continue or confront, with a few exceptions, can be turned into a reason to continue or confront. The real strength to be attained is hidden within the hurdles and pitfalls. If you want that strength then you have to overcome and defeat them. This strength will set you up to overcome further hurdles that will inevitably come your way. Look on stumbling blocks as challenges offering experiences that will build your mental and emotional strength.

Chapter Fourteen

Interviews

The following verbatim interviews are with a variety of people from different walks of life who have all gone through particularly fearful situations and lived to tell the tale. Their stories should be used as a source of knowledge and inspiration.

Interview 1:
Peter Mathews, Security Consultant

My first interview is with Peter Mathews, who spent just short of ten years in the intelligence corps with the Army and is now a consultant with a small security firm in London that deals with static security and the teaching and supplying of bodyguards.

Peter, will you please tell us a little about your work in the Army?
The first four years was the normal routine intelligence stuff, the security of the Army as well as the combat side of things, knowing your enemy, i.e., the Soviet Army and that sort of thing. I was then posted to a unit in Northern Ireland whose role was to keep a watch on what the bad guys were doing.

So that was very covert work?
Yeah. It was a very secretive operation.

How old are you now and how old were you when you arrived in Northern Ireland?
I'm 32 now and was 25 when I arrived in Ireland.

Because the work was so covert I guess there must have been a lot of fear involved.
Yes, it's the uncertainty of not knowing what was going to happen around the corner.

What was the hardest part of working undercover in such a volatile environment?
The anticipation, because you just never knew what was going to happen.

Like slow secretions of adrenalin?
Yes, did you see the footage of those two British soldiers that drove into the funeral cortege and were killed by some of the mourners at the funeral?

Yes I did, was the kind of thing that you, in your unit, had to do?
Yeah, but the problem with that was that although those two guys were attached to our unit, they had a limited amount of training. You know if that had been one of us, there would have been a lot more back-up and, more importantly, we wouldn't have been out in the ground that day because we would have known that there was a funeral. You forewarn yourself of what's happening.

So in your job, the worst-case scenario was death? Every day you had to face the possibility of being killed? How did you cope with that kind of constant fear?

Well, you tried to disguise the fact that you were scared and also disguise the fact that you were British. You would be sure to grunt if someone asked you a question, or if they asked you the time you'd answer by showing your wrist without a watch. If they heard your English accent you could be in trouble.

Do you think that the soldiers in the Army understood their own bodily reactions to conflict? Most people seem to mistake adrenalin, which is a natural reaction to confrontation of any kind, for fear.

No, I don't think they did. The only way I have come to understand it myself is from coming to your courses. Before that I just put it down to fear, anticipating confrontation and not knowing what was going to happen next.

Do you think that you were aware during anticipation of what it was you were actually afraid of?

No idea at all. We knew who the bad guys were but anything could happen and it was the anticipation of that that made you scared. A classic for instance: we were doing some work and one of our lads got circled by a group of young lads and they just closed in on him. Me and another soldier were paralleling in a side street and this guy just shouted out, 'Contact! Contact!' We ran to where we thought he was but we lost coms [communication] with him. He was being closed in by these four lads, we saw it all happening, and we just raced through these four or five guys and ran away with him.

So it was 'on top' straight away? Like adrenal dump?
Yeah, it was like, Christ, something's wrong here, let's get out of here.

Would it be fair to say that you wouldn't have been placed in the deep end like that straight away, there would have been some kind of build-up to it?
Yeah, well I was pushed into it quite quickly. I went over there originally as a collator, analysing all of the information that was coming in. They were short of opps [operatives] so I got selected as it were, did some limited training and then was out on the ground working.

Anticipation, or slow release adrenalin, was obviously the thing that you experienced most. How did you learn to cope with that? Did you just switch off?
A lot of the time the anticipation was almost excitement, I'd not done anything like it before. You were constantly thinking, 'I don't want to let myself down in front of my peers.' I'd been given this task and didn't want to let myself down and the people who had selected me for it. At the time I don't think I realised that it was fear, I just got on with it.

What about the 'WOW factor' [adrenal dump]? How did you react the first time you had it?
I think the first time the reactions were pretty swift, and then when I analysed it afterwards I thought, 'Jesus Christ, it's happened', but I was happy with myself and the way I performed.

What about aftermath, when you anticipated having to do the same again? How did you handle that?
I suppose it was worse really, you're more frightened.

A lot of people get hit with aftermath and they don't really understand it. A lot of people I've dealt with have an incident and cope well with it but then bottle out afterwards because of aftermath. Again, they mistake adrenalin for fear.
There is always the danger of situations reoccurring, but then it's your drills and your training that kick in. You react how you're trained to react, as we teach now on the bodyguard course. The thing was, then it was real, it was live, and your life was at stake, it wasn't a play situation, but you never ever got complacent, you always stayed on your guard.

Surely that kind of aftermath has to have an effect on the family unit?
Well, within our own unit there were thirty-nine or forty blokes and we'd regularly get a huge buzz by getting pissed and forgetting all about it.

And that was your release?
Yeah, there were blokes that didn't drink that much but occasionally we'd all have a good piss-up. But also there were incentives there to keep you going.

Like rewards?
Yeah. You'd get four or five days off in the mainland, the flights would all be paid for and everything.

Didn't you find it hard to switch off when you were on leave?
No, you were still geared up and it took twenty-four to forty-eight hours to wind down, and then when you landed back in the province you knew you were straight back into it, so there is that couple of days in between where things were nice and relaxed. Invariably you had that mental ability to switch it off and go, 'OK, am I in any danger at the moment? No, I shouldn't be.' However, you still keep your awareness to a certain level where you're not brain-dead but if something does happen then you can move up through your colour codes [codes of awareness].

So, to a degree, you're constantly switched on?
Yeah, you're not paranoid but you are switched on. I think if you ask anyone who's got a modicum of professionalism about them they'll all be the same, unless they're going around with their thumbs up their arses all the time.

Did you see people around you who couldn't cope with the fear?
Not really, there were set guidelines for how you were supposed to work. The first time you went out there [Ireland] was for a year, the subsequent posting was eighteen months and if you did a third tour it was two years. There was a regular thing with the Army psychiatrist to see how people were doing, though the Army psychiatrist was never much to go by, it was the old retired brigadier routine. But at the end of the day, you know, it was the buzz of the work because it was real time and was something you couldn't experience anywhere else. At someone's decision you could say, 'Right, we're going in', and people may die as a result

of that decision. It was a day to day war where nothing or everything could happen.

When times were ugly, how did you cope with your inner opponent?
When things got bad, if the morale was low amongst the lads, we would draw off each other. You draw strength from the other guys and they in turn would draw strength from you. It's that team spirit environment. But there were also times when you took yourself away to be by yourself and go through your own thoughts and say 'Yeah, that's OK, I can deal with that.'

You'd talk to yourself and tell yourself that things were going to be fine and that you could handle the situation?
Yeah, yeah.

Whenever I was faced with a situation I would look at the worst-case scenario and tell myself that if it happened I could handle it.
Yes, I'd agree with that. You have to accept the worst-case scenario but it is also important to be positive. If you start getting too negative and thinking that it's all going to go wrong, you'll end up being Neil out of *The Young Ones* [a very negative student from a TV sitcom]. If you're negative and depressive about it you're never going to get on. Another frightening thing is being interviewed by someone with a tape recorder [laughs].

Actually, it is frightening isn't it? Why do you think that is?
I don't know. Again, I suppose that it is the unexpected; you don't know what question you're going to be asked, it's not rehearsed, it's the anticipation.

I think that there is fear with most things that are new to us.
Yes there is.

How did you deal with killjoys, people in the unit who would try to lower the morale of the other lads?
Occasionally it was just a quiet chat in the corner.

Did you find as you reached higher positions and expanded that others around you seemed to resent your success?
There is not a lot that you can do about it. I have always worked with the philosophy that there will always be those who are above you who will shit on you and as you succeed there will always be those who will be jealous of that success. There is not a lot that you can do about it; that's life. But I've always said that if there is someone above who wants to shit on me then I'll always try to be good enough at what I do so that he can't do that, but if there are people behind me who are jealous then I'll set my standards and tell them to stop being jealous and do the same themselves.

But if they will not grow with you then you leave them behind?
Yes.

I found that as I started to expand and succeed, some of my friends seemed to resent me and I couldn't understand because you expect your mates to be pleased when you succeed. But a lot of people just aren't, are they? Perhaps they feel that you are leaving them behind.
It is the jealousy factor.

In terms of fear, what is the worst situation that you have found yourself in?
One time we were watching this lump of explosive from the top of a tower block, thirteen floors high with our observation point at the top. Every day we would have to go up in the lift to the OP [observation point]. For security reasons we would never just go straight to the thirteenth floor, every day we would get off at different floors, maybe the eighth or the ninth and then walk the last few flights by the stairs. Anyway, this one day I was travelling up the lift when it stopped, the doors opened and these three guys just appeared at the doorway in front of me. I thought that was it, I'd been pinged [caught]. Their [the IRA] method of operation would be to grab someone, rip his kit off him, put him in a boiler suit and a hood, then the back of a car and then completely out of the area.

That would be the last anyone had seen of them?
Yeah. Alive anyway.

What happened then?
I punched this guy out of the way, started to draw a weapon and punched the lift door closed. The lift doors were closing and the weapon was ready to fire. The door shut and I went off. Five minutes later I sat down and was shaking like a leaf.

Aftermath?
Yeah.

Would that have been your best situation as well?
Yeah, you've had the opportunity, someone has come across you and you've reacted to it positively, like you've been trained

to do. If I had hesitated for even one second they could have been all over me.

That split second can mean the difference between life and death.
Yes it can, definitely.

As you were exposed to more demanding situations did you draw strength from the victories that lay behind you? I would often use past experiences to pull me through a tricky situation, draw inspiration from it if you like. Like saying, 'I coped with all those other situations so I'm sure that I can cope with this.'
Yes, but I always found that as you get to the top of one tree you are then at the bottom of another, there's always a new challenge. But yes, I would draw on past experience and the knowledge gathered there to help me conquer new challenges.

I call it the progressive pyramid; when you reach the top of your fear pyramid it progresses on to another, it's all part of expanding.
Yes, I also used other people as examples to follow, and I'd say, 'Well, he did it like that and it worked for him, I'll try it like that myself.'

Do you find that although you dealt with fear in the combat zone, that confidence carried you through into civvy street and gave you confidence and standing in things peripheral to the Army?
Oh yeah, but it didn't stop you feeling fear, I would still feel it when dealing with new situations but I was able to cope because that's what the Army taught me to do. The fear might be getting out of the car to do a cold call as a salesman as opposed to facing a man with a gun, but it is fear nonetheless.

What I'm trying to show people with this book is that to be successful in any sphere of life you have to face adversity, because there is a cavernous hole between those who dream and those who take controlled risks. What advice would you offer anyone that wants to overcome fear and lead a braver, more prosperous life?
If the inside of you is scared of doing something, do it; that's the only way. But look at the consequences of what you are going to do and accept them before you do it.

Peter, thanks for your time.

Interview 2:
Andy Davis, Former Marine

From the age of seventeen, Andy Davis spent ten years in the Royal Marine Commandos where he experienced live fire fights as a soldier in the Falklands War and completed three tours of Northern Ireland. He left in 1990 and has been in the close protection industry ever since, working as a bodyguard and instructor to bodyguards. He also does a lot of surveillance work.

Andy, could you relate some of the instances you experienced as a Royal Marine which involved fear?
Yeah, I can tell you a classic example of fear and this will make you laugh. My first real experience of fear was when I had to travel down to Southampton as a teenager to take the medical to get in the Marines. That was something that I'd never come across before, and I said that it would make you laugh; the fear of stripping naked and being examined and this and that, and I shat myself, I was so embarrassed and very scared. I was on the train going down to Southampton from the north of England and I was very nervous.

But you still did it.
Oh yeah, definitely. I was already more or less accepted [into the Marines], I knew that my health was alright. But I was sitting on the train thinking, 'What am I doing here?' and when I got there I went through the hearing test, the eye test, taking your clothes off and various other things. I experienced all the effects of adrenalin; you know, the

sweaty palms and shaking legs. Yeah, I was very nervous. Obviously it wouldn't bother me now because I'm always taking my bloody clothes off.

So it was really the fear of the unknown?
Yeah, it was nothing to do with fighting or shooting or anything like that, it was just something that I'd never had to do before.

How did you control the inner opponent way back in those early days when you wanted to get off the train and go home?
In that particular incident, Geoff, I couldn't really tell you, it was something that I've got that has just got stronger and stronger. But it was definitely brought out in the Royal Marines training. It's an old adage and a lot of people say it but it's true; no one in my family thought that I could do it and that inspired me to succeed.

I had eight months there [in basic training] and it was the hardest eight months that I have ever had, I've never found anything comparable to it since. If we were doing something particularly hard, normally physical because that is what it is nearly all about, I would wake up really nervous. Like the assault courses; I thought, 'If I drop out, I'm out of the Marines', and there was no way I was going to go home and say that I'd failed. That was my thing at the time, I wasn't going to go home and say that I couldn't do it. And that's what I did. I used that to inspire me on. If I had a thirty-mile run to do, that was my goal.

At that time, being a Royal Marine really did mean something, it was what, a year and a half before the Falklands, in 1981, they weren't that well known and had a reputation like the

Parachute Regiment, and I wanted to be a part of it. I wanted to be one of those hard men, simple as that, that was my light at the end of the tunnel.

So you had a definite goal right from the start?
Oh yeah. If you've got nothing to aim for you're always thinking, 'Why am I doing this, what's it all for?'

I remember reading about a group of people that tried to get in to 23 SAS (TA) and it was only the ones who really knew what they wanted from the regiment that got through. The others had no real goal, no road map, so when things got a little ugly the inner opponent would click in and ask them, 'Why are you doing this, why are you putting yourself through so much pain, what is at the end of this for you?' And because they didn't really know the answers they couldn't fight back and invariably dropped out from selection.

I think a lot of people are doing it for the wrong reasons, like a lot of people that go on the door. Initially they like the image and all the fame that they think goes with the job but when they get there and find out what it's really about they don't stay there for very long. You've got to know why you're there and have a goal, then you've got something to fight for.

They say that success is the best revenge, so if you think that people are expecting you to fail you can use that to fuel the fight. When you struggled in the early days of being a Marine, when you didn't know what it was all about, you controlled your inner opponent by thinking about the people who said you'd fail.
Yes, without a doubt, but without knowing it. At the time I didn't understand the mechanics of it all, I just knew that

I wasn't going to go back to my family and say I couldn't handle it.

So you just found a natural solution?
Yeah. I just told myself that I wasn't going to quit.

Do you use the same doggedness now when things get ugly or when training gets hard?
I'll go till I drop.

Is that because you've learned to understand and control the inner opponent?
Yeah. And it's [his will] got stronger.

Would you say that it got stronger because you've constantly met things head on?
Yeah, I would think so. In fact I can't think of any other way that it would get stronger. You get stronger as soon as you confront something different, it might not be a dangerous thing, it might be like Peter was saying about having a fear of a cold call in sales. I mean, I confronted the same kind of thing three years ago when I first started lecturing on the basic selection courses.

That can be frightening.
Up in front of forty people and I'm stood there in a suit and I'm trying to portray this image of being a bodyguard and I was a bag of shit, I was literally a bag of nerves. I'd never lectured before in my life, even when I was in the Marines, but I knew the subject matter so I just went ahead and did it. Then after I'd done it a couple of times I began doing the higher lectures

on the week course and teaching on the ranges, and it just goes up, but every time there is a another step and when you get there you just think, 'yeah, I can do it', you take a deep breath and get on with it.

Like the fear pyramid, you're not going from step one to step ten, you are gradually climbing the pyramid one step at a time.
Yes, you're better doing it gradually.

And you use each past victory to inspire you through the next steps?
Yeah, you must have done the same yourself, Geoff.

Yes, when I've reached sticking points in the past I just tell myself, 'You've done it before Geoff, you can do it again,' and I remind myself of all my past victories and that they were no different. I got past them and I'll get past this.
Previous victories help to give you faith in yourself. But the thing is, like I said before, there is always something new to confront; anyone who thinks they're at the top of the tree should have a good look around them.

I call it the progressive pyramid, when you reach the pinnacle of one pyramid you start at the bottom of another. There is always going to be something in life to go for, even though it will be at a much higher level. The feeling of fear does not go away as long as you are expanding and growing, but you do learn to captain and control it. The most important and fundamental factor is that you learn to recognise what the feelings are and why they are there and that they will aid your response to any given instance.
I think I've got that.

Yes you have, that's why you are so determined and so strong because you have it going for you where most people have it going against them. If you could have understood a little more about your own body as a young Marine I'm sure that it would have helped you a lot. Many people give in and never reach their full potential in life, not because they are cowards but because they mistake adrenalin for fear.

I do think though, that I have always had that determination, and although I never knew or understood the feelings I wouldn't give in to them. I think it might have been because in the Marines you're taught to act as a unit so you draw off other people and other people draw off you. For instance, if you are near or under the governor, whoever he might be, you pick up something from him, you get something off people like that don't you? Then as you go on a bit more and build confidence you become that person, or one of those people, and people pick it up off you. Then you get a little buzz out of that as well.

Going back to the Falklands Andy, what was your worst experience of anticipation, or what I call slow release adrenalin?

The worst anticipation and slow release adrenalin that I've had was a scenario in Northern Ireland on a particular tour a few years ago. It was the last time that I was out there and I was working in South Armagh. In South Armagh, the particular place that I was in you couldn't go anywhere by vehicle, it was all by helicopter because all the roads were mined. So you had to go through the people like Peter [Mathews] who worked undercover.

We were informed by them that the IRA had bought two SAM missiles that had been imported into the country, SAM being the Surface to Air Missile which is a hand held thing used with the specific aim of bringing the helicopters down. Now this threat went on for about a month I should think, and bearing in mind that you were in a helicopter sometimes six to eight times a day, flying to different places, patrolling, out again in a helicopter and being picked up again. That was a feeling, the same type of thing that you're talking about, but it was slow, over the period of a month, but happening every time that you went up. Again, I wouldn't mistake that for fear, because in a way if it did happen it would happen and there was nothing that you could do about it, it was out of your control.

Anyway, when you're looking out of a helicopter, especially a Lynx helicopter, for anything that might come your way, not that you could do anything about it, well I think that we all drew off each other then. I was a bit older then, it was about five or six years ago and people looked up to me and drew off me, and I think you find that when you know people are relying on you, and most of the young lads are trying to take something off you, it makes you strong because you can't afford to show any weakness at all.

You've a position to hold.
You have to maintain that no matter how you feel. I think in a way some of it is bluff as well, because I'm still feeling scared inside but I can't show it to anyone else.

Like the duck syndrome?
Yeah, exactly like that. But that particular situation was definitely a slow release.

I don't class any of the situations as fear, per se, I view them as different forms of adrenalin. Sometimes the body will release adrenalin even when you may be just viewing a situation, like witnessing a robbery even though you may not be involved in it directly.

Well I can relate to that myself, because on that particular tour of Northern Ireland we got six days off to go home and see the family. Myself and my four-man team had just come back from our four-day leave and were waiting at a particular heliport in South Armagh to fly back from there to our own camp. Whilst we were waiting they [the IRA] shot down the helicopter before mine. They shot it down. They had a flatbed lorry with a point five Browning.

When they shot the helicopter down we were in what they call the buzzard room which is on the helipad. You have like an operations room where they control all the helicopters, and this is the busiest heliport in Europe, the second busiest in the world. We actually listened to it on the radio as it was shot down and I got adrenalin straight away. Not because of the fact that it might have been the helicopter that I was going on because it wasn't intended for us anyway, it was delivering something else, but listening to the helicopter pilot giving a contact report was the coolest thing I've ever heard in my life, it was like something off *Top Gun*. As he was spinning and going down the IRA came down off the top of the hill to finish them off. But the Army had a reaction team there so they lost no one, purely to the skill of the pilot. But just listening to that gave me an adrenalin rush and I was fifteen miles away, I wasn't even involved.

What was the worst situation that you can remember involving fast release adrenalin or adrenal dump?
I've never had that with anything that ever happened to me in the Marines. I've had it on the door. This was probably due to the fact that we were always in code yellow [a state of anticipation], because we were always anticipating a contact [action] we were never really taken by surprise.

Tell us about the door [working as a bouncer].
We were working in a particular part of Somerset where it was renowned for being particularly rough, it was just one of those places. I'd been scared on the door there knowing that it was going to kick off [trouble was going to start]. As you know yourself an incident had gone off and we were expecting a come-back on that, we were expecting a revenge attack.

This would be aftermath?
Yeah, well we were all out-of-town doormen. We were brought in because the last lot of doormen couldn't cope with the trouble but we didn't do any better, and we'd have fighting every night. We'd have the situations with the bats [baseball bats] and everything else... and I'd be scared. I knew that fighting was going to happen and I could control the adrenalin in myself but I didn't have any control over anything that was going on around me. In my eyes, out of the other six doormen, two shouldn't have been there anyway and I had no faith in anything behind me, which I found a bit soul-destroying – when I'm prepared to give them everything that I've got but I knew that I wouldn't get the same back.

You can't win in a situation like that unless you've got the right backing from good doormen.

I never won anything on the door. If someone has recognised me a couple of weeks later, that's different, it's one on one and I'm quite happy with that, you know, win or lose because I know that I'll give it everything that I've got. Now, compare that to maybe a fire fight, and again, not quoting a particular incident, but we've been anticipating it for a month, we're then being shot at and you don't feel anything at all. You get adrenalin but I've never mistaken that for fear and never seen anyone around me mistake that for fear. I put that down to the training, definitely the training.

When you come out of it though and you get, well I won't say shaking, but you know when you've had a good one on the door and you get that pallor of skin and you sit down and you're like that [looks relieved]. And our release is to go out and have a good piss-up. [Points to me] You don't drink so you'd probably go and do a hard session of training to get your release, but in the forces we like to blow out by having a few beers. In Ireland you can't do that so it's still in you, because you're not allowed to drink, then I'd train all the time to get it out of me.

It has to be released in some way.

If you keep it there you're going to suffer for that. If you don't release that kind of aftermath it starts affecting the people around you. As far as training and that goes, and I'm very inconsistent with my training, I'll blast it out for a few weeks and then do nothing for a month, but definitely, if I'm not training at home it definitely affects myself and my girlfriend. I don't get nasty-nasty but I'll say things and afterwards I'll think 'Why did I say that?' And yet she'll say to me 'Why don't you go for a run?' and she knows if I go for a run I always go early in the morning. I'll come back, have a shower and I'm like, 'Isn't it a lovely day?' All that adrenalin that's been hanging around inside me has gone and I feel great.

It gets all the shit out of the system?
Yeah, I always feel better for it.

When you found yourself in a state of anticipation, what did you do to take your mind off whatever it was that you were anticipating?
If you think about the kind of situations that I was talking about in the Marines, we were always busy anyway, so we never really had time to dwell on it. They [the officers] always made sure that we had something to do. But also you're confident with the lads around you, and we'd be training, and we'd talk about things like that and we'd joke about it. What I always used to find was sarcasm and taking the piss, which is something that I never came across with girlfriends and wives when speaking to them: 'Oh yeah, if they blow us up today you'll get some money out of it,' you know, the piss-taking thing which you probably did yourself on the door, 'Oh we're expecting so and so in tonight, I might get beaten to a pulp but, you know, shit happens.' I think that by talking about it, not worrying about it, you can see the difference.

So, inadvertently, by using black humour, what you are doing is looking at the worst-case scenario and then accepting that you can handle it by joking about it.
Yeah, I suppose so.

If you take it too seriously you'll probably fall apart.
Yeah, and then you won't be able to do what you are there to do, whether you're on the door or out on patrol, you just can't do it.

It seems the same in any environment where there is an element of danger; the door, the Army, bodyguarding, you overcome the constant threat with humour.
I don't personally ever want to work out of this environment, I love it. I may have to, but whilst you stay in this line of work you're always going to get that kind of camaraderie that you don't get anywhere else.

I must admit I've been involved in hundreds of fights and yet one of the bravest things that I ever did was leaving the factory. I was so scared to leave because I kept thinking that my whole world was going to fall apart if I didn't get another job, or if I lost or didn't like the new job.
I can relate to that, Geoff, because, although it's not quite the same now, when I left the forces in 1990 you couldn't get a more secure job, I left the securest job you could get in the world. As my time was coming up to leave I was looking for things, applying for jobs and was getting no results at all and that was really scary shit. I didn't have the responsibilities that I've got now with the baby and the house, but I was leaving a lot of friends and a very close-knit environment, you were protected, there were no mortgages, nothing. You get X amount of money a month, travelled the world, didn't have to look for meal or do any washing, everything was done for you.

The ultimate comfort zone really.
Yeah, exactly. Then suddenly it's civvy street. What's in civvy street? I don't know. And I got this job purely by chance

and then I got into civvy street. But I was working on the motorways for what, about twelve months and I earned a lot of money. There were a lot of lads working there as well, but what I found was, when we're talking about the male environment like the door and the forces, that it wasn't the same sense of humour on the roads as I'd known in the forces. They thought I was a nutter, they couldn't get their heads round me. They all thought that I was crazy. To me I was just doing, you know, things for a laugh, not fighting or anything like that, but I really found it hard to relate to sometimes. So what I'm saying there, Geoff, is that was frightening, leaving the safe environment of the armed forces, I mean I didn't have to leave, I could have stayed there for another fourteen years.

When I started to expand myself and achieve things I found that it caused resentment to some of the people around me. Did you ever experience this kind of bad feeling?

To be honest I didn't, and really I resent the people who resented you, I never experienced that kind of thing. But you're very astute Geoff. You know the main thing as well, all you've done is what they want to do, but they haven't got the bottle or whatever to do it. We both know that, don't we?

Yeah, it's true, but by the same count it's very disappointing that people can't be happy for you to do well. You hear of a lot of people saying, 'Oh yeah, Geoff Thompson's changed since he published that book [Watch My Back], *you can't talk to him any more,' which is ludicrous, I haven't changed at all.*

I've lost count of the amount of people that have said I've changed since I've left the Marines.

Lots of people would like to be doing what you're doing now [bodyguarding] but they haven't got the bottle to even try.
There are a lot of jealous people about; you can't afford to worry about them.

Just going back to the Marines, Andy, how did they help you to overcome the fears associated with basic training?
Well, heights have never been a good thing with me. I don't think I'm scared of heights but I'm wary, and the first time I had to go down the death slide, 180-feet high with all your kit on, bearing in mind that I was only 17 years old, I remember looking down and thinking, 'Fucking hell!' I mean, people do refuse to go down. I remember thinking 'why am I here?' You can't really explain it and then you just think 'fuck it,' and then you go. Something in my head just says 'deal with it.'

My pet hate is abseiling and I had a bad experience of that, of breaking a foot coming down the rope. They have a thing called free abseiling which is out of a helicopter where you've got nothing to bounce off, all you do is lean out of the helicopter at 90 degrees, look down and off you go. Now I've done that before on the skid of a helicopter and leant out and been really scared. You say about the difference between fear and adrenalin or them both being the same but I was scared. But again you've got people on the ground who know you, and you've got lads who are waiting their turn and I know they're thinking the same as me, I know they are. Some cope with it better or they bluff it better.

Do you take solace in the fact that everyone else is feeling the same?
Yes, definitely.

What about the people that refuse or cannot summon up the courage to go down the death slide or abseil from a helicopter?
I've had lads that have refused the first time and the second, but then they've done it and I've got nothing but admiration for them. Especially in the Marines when you're doing something like the commando test, when they do get a second chance, but then they've got a week to think about it. They know that next Thursday they've got one more chance, but what do they do in that week when they know they've got to do something that they've already bottled – the people that do that, I mean what do you think of them? What amazing people. Whereas other people have gone for it again and said, 'No, I can't do it.' And they're out of there, that's them, that's their chance gone, they won't get another one. I always think, like with the death slide for instance, that if I don't do it now I'll be up here again next week so I might as well get it over with.

They say that real power is not in making others do as you want, it is in making yourself do what you want. I have found from experience that the hardest fight has not been with an exterior thing, it has been with myself.
That's the only battle to win in my eyes.

Someone once asked me which was my hardest fight and I told them that it was with myself.
Did you win that one? [laughs]

[Laughs] I lost a few times in the early days, I have to tell you, but once I had won the internal battle I felt like I could take on the world. What I'm trying to show people though, Andy, is that you don't just arrive in a

position of power, there is a lot of hard work involved, and anyone who is willing to take on that workload can achieve the same goals. Anyone can become strong but they have to fight the fight. I've come from a position of weakness and arrived at a position of power; so can everyone else.
Oh yeah, I've got to agree with you.

As a conclusion, what advice would you offer to people who want to learn to overcome their fears?
All fears seem to be comparable; somebody might find responsibility just as stressful as me going down the death slide, or you fighting so-and-so, we're all in the same position, we're like, 'Fucking hell, I don't want to be here.'

It's true. I can show you a man who has fought four men in a blood and snot fight and yet he couldn't handle the responsibility of a mortgage, it frightened him to death, to the extent that it broke up his marriage. So whilst the two seem unrelated they're not; they both evoke fear, the difference being that this man could understand the fear involved with fighting four men and could handle it well, but when the same kind of feeling came in the guise of responsibility he didn't know how to fight it, so he succumbed. Realistically, if you fight four men you might die, but what's the worst-case scenario if you can't pay the mortgage? You're hardly going to end up on the streets, not in this day and age, but even if you did it's got to be better than dying at the hands of four attackers.

What I'm trying to say is that if my friend had understood his own bodily reactions to the thought of the responsibility tied to a mortgage and the way to fight it, he'd have handled it. Most people panic through ignorance rather than fear.

Actually, I can understand that because I have handled fire fights in the Falklands without too much of a problem but one of my biggest fears was on a course here, what, a year ago next month when my girlfriend rang me up and said 'I'm pregnant'. That just totally fucked me up, it was just out of the blue. Bearing in mind that I'd been seeing Kim then for a year, the pregnancy was a pure accident, and I was just scared, I got adrenalin straight away. I said to her, 'You're taking the piss aren't you?' She said, 'No, ring me back later.' You can ask Peter, I said, 'You won't believe this', and I told him and he started laughing which made me feel loads better [laughs].

Again, this wasn't any of your fighting and fire fights and things but I was just like that; thirty years old, I've always run away from things like that and I've had several girlfriends. It's the fear of responsibility, I like to go out for my beer, I like to do my own thing and I've always liked living by myself and being by myself. And I was scared, the responsibility is there in your face.

I got some advice from Peter and then I rang her back and said, 'Yeah, we'll go for it.' That made the whole thing then to hear her response and I've never regretted it since. That was confrontation again, it was adversity.

Your final advice for people struggling with adversity, Andy?

Well, all you can do really is confront it; it's like the old adage of speculate to accumulate. But if you're not prepared to do that, and there is always a little bit of risk involved in everything, whether it is leaving an old job, starting a new job, or going for this or going for that, if you don't want to go for it then you're going to stay exactly where you are now. If you want to go for something just go for it, we've all done that in different degrees. Just step into it. It's like the thing you say, it could be about fighting or just changing your job – what have you got to lose?

And the risks are never as great as you think, are they?
I always look at the worst scenario, which is what you do, I think that's the best thing to do, and you rarely come across that anyway, anything in between and you've got a bonus.

Andy, thanks for your time.

Interview 3:
Pat Leemy, Pro Boxing Trainer

Pat is a pro boxing trainer who has been in the game for about thirty-five years both as amateur and professional. At the moment he is looking after Jim MacDonnell. He has also trained world title holders in the professional arena.

Having been an avid boxing fan I have always been aware that in the boxing ring there are no real losers, anyone who steps into the ring to battle with another fighter, to me, is a winner all day long. And there are lessons learned in losing that cannot be learned in any other way, and they are very important lessons. Losing is just another set of experiences.
Yes, exactly. Life's all about winning and losing Geoff, whether it's your job or crossing the road. I mean, if you get to the other side then you've won, if you get knocked over by a No. 79 bus you've lost. It's all about winning and losing.

Do you find that it is the same no matter what it is in life that you want to achieve, success in your career, relationship or overcoming fears?
You only get out of life what you put into it, and that's true whether it be sport, marriage, whatever it is. Older people say that you reap what you sow and that's true. In sport it is exactly the same – if you try and cut corners and cheat you fail, and even if you become the champion you've still not really become a champion within yourself.

It doesn't necessarily mean a thing does it?
Nothing. Because you know that you could be that much better. And that's what we all strive to be, the very best of our

own ability. As a trainer that's my aim. I see what the guy's got and if he's never going to be a top-class boxer, even though he may think he is, your job is to go along with him and help him to achieve the very best that he can with his given ability.

By achieving your own personal best you have already won haven't you, Pat?
Exactly.

Whether or not that is the world title or an amateur's bout in the local church hall, you're already a winner.
Yes. And then you ask the question of your boxer, why do you want to go down that road, why do you want to go into the ring? Nine times out of ten it is not just about the money, it's about getting something out of their life. They might not be the best achievers in regard to academia and they might not be the best kid in the class at school. God moves in mysterious ways; what you may lack in one way is compensated in another and this is why a lot of guys excel in sport. They might not be the brightest guys in the world but they excel in their sport, because they know that God's given them this gift, and it is a gift.

I mean you can get to a certain level in sport and you can see this guy's improved but you can get another guy coming along who's never attempted it before and he's a natural, he's been given this gift. It's all about finding that inner part of us, what our pluses are. We already know what our minuses are, we come across them every day of the week; we want to find out what our pluses are. And sometimes it might take a prison sentence where you've got the seclusion and the peace and quiet to know that you can paint.

That's the real journey isn't it, finding out what you are really capable of. With people like Jimmy Boyle and John McVicar, both former criminals, it took prison sentences for them to realise their hidden talents for writing. I have found that the reason why most people do not achieve is because they do not dig and find their own treasure trove.

And you know what, sometimes you may be digging for that crown jewel and find a ruby on the way. In other words, I knew my ability as a boxer, I had say thirty to thirty-five amateur fights, never turned professional, I was a pure amateur. I knew the level that I was going to get to and I knew that I wasn't going to get above that. You know, one day I woke up and said, 'Well look, this is the best that I'm going to be, I can live with that.' And now I look back and I can smile about it because I was, as a young man, probably more honest to myself than most young kids are. So while I was looking for that crown jewel I realised that I had a gift for passing on to others what I had learned. And that's the beauty of this game, you never stop learning. I'm 53 years of age and I feel like I'm just scratching the surface. There is so much out there to learn, like when the Americans came over I learned their approach from them. You can never stop learning. There is so much, and any guy that says he knows it all is a fool; he's a liar and he's a fool.

What surprises me is that most people go through their whole lives and learn more about the engines in their cars than about their own bodies and their own bodily reactions to confrontation. They still panic when they feel fear because they don't understand that it is a natural bodily function, and yet they could perhaps tell you what is wrong with a car just by the sound of the engine. That's what this book is predominantly about, teaching people to understand and so subsequently control their own body and mind. How do you deal with a boxer who is suffering with the fear syndrome?

What you try and do is prepare them for that day and I don't give a shit who you are, everyone feels nerves, it's learning how to control them, that's the art. Controlling the nerves so that they don't affect your performance on the night of the fight, and I think the best way of doing that is to do what we're doing now, sitting down and talking about it. You can get technical, give them a book to read or let them watch a video and this that and the other, and it will all help, after all, knowledge is power, as you said Geoff. But to my mind the best thing that you can do is, if you can, sit down, and this is where it is important to be able to get close to people, and you might start talking about the weather but gradually the subject will get around to a particular sport or problem; in this case boxing. My sport is boxing, and when the subject does come up it inevitably turns to how the boxer feels and his insecurities about getting into the ring. You explain to him all about the negatives, about how he is going to feel scared and that it is natural. Once you start telling him about all the positive things he's going to get for stepping into that ring, into his fears if you like, that will put things into perspective for him. Just the fact that he has talked to you about how he feels makes him feel a hell of a lot better, and how? Because he's probably been carrying it around with him for a long time. Once you start working on the positives he'll start forgetting about the negatives.

So what you want to do is to take him out of this arena where he feels fear and you want to take him into the arena where he feels confident, you also remind him that at all times you must respect the fear and learn to live with it, learn to cope with it and learn to realise that it's that feeling of adrenalin that the body needs. There is only one mechanism that makes the body work at its best and that's fear.

So the fighter takes a lot of solace from the fact that you and the other fighters are saying, 'We feel that too, that's natural, that's your strength.'
Oh yeah, definitely.

I think the worst thing is when you don't talk to anyone else about how you feel and then think that you are the only person in the world feeling fear. Jimmy [MacDonnell] was telling me that when he first started in the fight game he was that worried about the fact that he was feeling fear that he wondered whether or not he was cut out for it. Then Chris Pyat [world title holder] told him that the feelings he was experiencing were natural and that he had to learn to go with the flow. After that there was no stopping him.
Nowadays boxers are opening up to each other, you know they've got so much in common; they've all tasted victory, they've all tasted defeat, sometimes they might have even won the bout but they've lost within themselves, and now they're sharing their experiences.

You talk to Nigel Benn. Nigel's first job in boxing was when he had this terrible, I mean an out and out battle with fear, but when he won that battle he became a different fighter. He even went over to see Herby [Hide, former world heavyweight champion] when he was having the biggest fight of his life with Riddick Bo. He went to Herby's hotel room and sat down with him and said, 'Herby, I know what you're going through, I know how you're feeling, I've been there, I was there last week [when Nigel successfully defended his title against McAlan]. Everyone said that I had no chance, everyone said that I was a loser but I knew, I knew deep down that I could win.' And what Nigel did was sit and talk to Herby and pass on that feeling and that determination to him.

In that case Herby didn't win the bout but he showed a hell of a lot of courage in defeat. There's not a lot of people who'll get up six times, I mean he could have taken the million quid and run after the first knock down but he didn't, because he was probably thinking, 'Nigel got put down in the first round, he was out of the fight in the first round', but Nigel being the character that he is and the determination that he showed, went on to win the fight by a knockout.

But getting back to the point, this is where boxers can help each other and this is why when I see two boxers talking to each other, I'll slip into the background and let them discuss everything because I know that eventually the conversation is going to come back to what they do best, boxing, and therefore they can learn from each other.

You know the old male has always been this guy who wants to create an image of a tough guy who hasn't got any feelings. You know and I know that sometimes when things go wrong and we get home to our solitary little bedrooms we all sit down and have a little cry. There is not a man living that hasn't sat down at some time and had a good cry. So when one boxer tells another boxer what he went through, whether it was in winning or whether it was in defeat, once they understand these feelings they no longer become a weight on their shoulders. The weight is lifted because they say, 'If someone like Ali can come back from defeat and take the world title for the third time, then I can come back from defeat; one defeat isn't the end of the world.'

I remember Ali as an amateur; he had tremendous problems with fear, the same as Tyson did. Ali's trainer told him that he should always confront those things that he feared.
Yeah, Tyson used to get physically sick before a fight, even ran away a couple of times. But it's the same as anything – once you've done it a few times and gained a bit of confidence it gets easier and easier. Not to the stage where you become complacent, you have to always maintain a healthy respect for fear, like fire, like water, respect it. Respect it, control it and don't let it control you.

As an experienced man, Pat, what advice would you offer to people in life, not just in boxing, who are failing to achieve because of fear?
I think the solution is there for everyone, whatever problem they've got in life. Whether they're an alcoholic, drug addict, or a sportsman who's struggling with his fears, they've got to talk about it, get it out in the open, don't bottle it up. I mean if you bottle it up all it's going to do is eat away at you and it will destroy you. There's only one way that you can let go of something and that is to talk about it. Also at some point you have to confront that fear, but talk first, you can't confront it until it is out in the open. Let it out, share it with someone sensible, someone that you can talk to and then confront it. You'll be surprised how the people that you talk to will say 'I've had that feeling, this is how I overcame it'. That really helps, to know that others have felt the same as you.

Thanks very much Pat, that was brilliant.
You're welcome.

Interview 4:
Jim MacDonnell, Boxing Trainer

Jim was a former double ABA boxing champion (once 'officially', says Jim laughing, the other he lost on a 'dodgy' decision), Commonwealth Games silver medallist (amateur) and United Nations gold medallist in Austria. Professionally, he is a Southern Area champion, undefeated European champion and beat three out of the five world champions that he fought, including Barry McGuigan. He fought an epic battle with Azumo Nelson. Jim also trains up-and-coming professional boxers.

Jim, how do you deal with pre-fight fear, the anticipation of confrontation?
Directly before a fight in the changing room there's a buzz of anticipation, when it's right on you. But I think before that stage arrives I've already prepared myself by dealing with my friend, which is what I call fear, which I have studied in great detail for many years and have learned to understand, so I never let it overcome me. I think a lot of fighters who can't handle it [fear] can be world champions in the gym but can't produce it on the night. The reason being, not because they are any less a fighter but they can't deal with the inner opponent.

Leading up to the fight, once I'm physically ready, which I normally am two weeks before a fight, I go to work on the mental side of it. On the night of the contest I get a bit of anticipation before I get into the ring but I've dealt with everything else beforehand; the walk to the ring, sitting in the changing room, the trainer putting my bandages on, gloving up [putting on the boxing gloves], the introductions, the announcements of the weight. It's all been done; it's all been rehearsed like a play, so consequently when I arrive there [at the stadium] I feel very cool, very calm and very collected.

Even before the biggest fight of my life, which was for the world featherweight title, I left instructions that I didn't want anyone at all in the changing room an hour before the fight; no visits, no good luck messages. I just wanted to be on my own to deal with what had to be dealt with, which was the mental side. And I remember Barry Hearn, who was promoting the show, coming in about twenty minutes before the fight and saying that he thought I must have water for blood going through my veins because I was so cool. That was the actual statement that he made because he couldn't believe my temperament, but that was because I knew how to deal with the situation.

The reason you were so calm was because you had already dealt with the fight before you even entered the ring, with visualisation?
Yes, that's right. As an amateur I suffered, when I was a younger guy I couldn't understand the feelings that I was experiencing, I wondered whether I should be in the fight game. I used to go to fights and I would dread being there. I'd feel great once I got into the ring and box and afterwards I'd feel sensational, but the actual lead up to it I used to hate. Sleepless nights, pain in my lower back, all sorts of things that I now realise are part of the fear factor, and now I do understand it I just feel I've graduated in that department.

You talked about people that could fight brilliantly in the gym and yet they couldn't deliver the goods on fight night. Do you think that this lack of understanding about fear is mostly to blame?

Yeah, I know it's the reason, because I've worked with fighters in the gym who could match me punch for punch but they couldn't perform the same in a pressure situation such as a big show. Even as an amateur I worked with a guy who they eventually put in the ring to compete against me in the ABAs. The original agreement was that they wouldn't put us in against each other because we were in the same camp and because we were the same weight we sparred against each other.

As good as this lad was in the gym, when it was for real, with little gloves on, the fight only went one round, and it was for that reason. And yet in the gym you wouldn't have known who was the better fighter, but I was a stronger person in the mind and I think that was the actual difference when he competed.

Professionally, you see a lot of guys who go into the sport and everyone thinks that they fall short because when it comes to it, not necessarily at the beginning of their career when it's only eight rounds and their class gets them through, but when it gets to the higher level when the fight game becomes eighty per cent mental, they get to the situation where they can't deal with the pressure. The only pressure is inside your mind, you're making the pressure inside your own head. There's that old statement that Frank Bruno often uses and it's a true statement, 'if you can't stand the heat, get out of the kitchen.'

You've obviously got to get your conditioning right and have the ability to perform, but even with all the talent in the world, if you can't beat the man on the inside then you can't beat the man on the outside.
Yeah. Absolutely. Because I think physical and mental conditioning go hand in hand, part of the preparation for a fight is talking to yourself. I'll explain to myself why I'm doing certain training sessions, when I get out of bed in the morning I've got to say to myself, 'I'm getting out of bed to kick ass', because that's the reason why I'm going out on the road [running].

So you're talking to your inner opponent?
Yeah, on a regular basis. One of the things that I do, I did it before the Barry McGuigan fight, people thought it was weird what I wanted to do, but I wanted to be isolated for ten days and I went and stayed up in the Lake District. I checked my own weight, I found a gym that I could work out in. I just wanted to be with myself because I knew on the night of the fight that was exactly what I was going to be, on my own. That was something that I personally wanted to do, and I felt comfortable with it and really, like lived with myself.

Could you just enlarge on why you felt you needed solitude?
I got to the stage where everyone I was meeting in the street were pulling faces and saying 'you're fighting McGuigan, you've got no chance, silly move,' that kind of thing. All the press were being negative about my chances of winning the fight so I didn't want to read any press leading up to the fight because it was all negative.

You've got two departments, you've got negative and you've got positive and I think it depends on which one you want to build on. I only wanted the positives going into my mind, which is PMA: Positive Mental Attitude. But everything that was in the press, which I read after the contest, was derogatory so I didn't bother reading it, I'd sit down and go through the positives.

The positives were 'If you beat Barry McGuigan you're gonna get X amount of money for your next fight, you're gonna go on to fight for the world title and you're gonna have fame, you're gonna have this, you're gonna have that, you're gonna get sponsorship.' The negative side of it was, 'You're gonna go back to work, you're gonna be told that you weren't good enough in the first place.' I felt like the only way that I could surpass that feeling was not to listen to my mates saying 'you can't do it'. I really had to listen to myself saying that I could do it. That's why I wanted to be away from all the people giving me negative vibes.

People are like that aren't they Jim? They are almost willing you to fail. They think that you are pretentious for getting into the ring with someone like McGuigan. They seem to think that you are getting above your station. So they try to drag you down by being negative. And when you complain about their attitude they say that they're just trying to keep your feet on the floor. So your way of coping with these people was to simply separate yourself from them?

Yeah, completely. I find in boxing in general you get a lot of people who aren't clued up on the kind of things that we're talking about just now, and that is no disrespect to them, they just don't understand what they're talking about. People said to me before the McGuigan fight, 'You've got no chance'. Even before the fight was on the cards people said to me, 'I bet you wouldn't like to fight Barry McGuigan'.

What a lot of people don't realise is that I had two grand on myself to beat McGuigan at five to two, which is the only fight that I've ever bet on, because my inner confidence was total, absolutely total, and the fight itself was so one-sided, I think I'd psyched McGuigan out before we got in the ring. We played a mind game with each other and it got a little bit nasty in the lead up but that's part of the game. Even in the pre-fight interviews when we were told to shake hands for the cameras, I deliberately refused on the grounds that I looked at that as a sign of weakness and I wasn't prepared to stand there and do it. It wasn't because I didn't like him as a person, it was just a mind game. I was winning and I stuck with it.

You were saying that McGuigan was a beaten man before he even got into the ring, you'd beaten his inner opponent with the pre-fight mind games.

Yeah, I met McGuigan at a press conference to announce the fight and we shook hands and he tried to break my hand with a handshake. From that day on, every time we went to a press conference (we had eleven all together in the lead up to the fight which was a 12,000 sell-out eventually), there was a needle between us. During the press conference a week before the fight the press asked the question, 'Why have you and McGuigan fallen out?' Actually, come to think of it, two weeks before that at another press conference I'd told the press that I was going to knock McGuigan out and end his career and they were invited to a party after the fight: the Barry McGuigan retirement party. McGuigan really bit the bullet on that one and lost it. He actually threatened to knock me out there and then, he got restrained from attacking me. I remember saying, 'Let him go, let's get it on.' And I meant it.

A few minutes after that the cameras and the press said, 'This is bad for boxing, fellas, let's just shake hands and get a nice photo for the Manchester Evening Press and for the TV.' McGuigan actually put his hand out to shake hands but even then I was playing with his mind and I refused point blank. I said, 'I don't want to shake hands with nobody,' and I pursued with that right the way through because we had two or three press conferences after that. When McGuigan was asked a week before the fight why there was so much animosity he told them that I'd said something that had really riled him and he'd never been so grieved and upset by what someone had said. He said that he didn't want to state what it was but all that it was, Geoff, was that I'd threatened to knock him out and invited the press to his retirement party.

McGuigan said that he was going to teach me to respect a former world champion and that he was going to be world champion again. He said that he was in the best shape of his career, he was training with Jimmy Tibbs who he said had brought out the best in him and that he was fighting better than ever. He'd had three sparring partners in camp who were all forced to go home early and he said that I was going to go the same way.

On the morning of the fight the press held a conference for a final statement and McGuigan showed a sign of weakness then. He said that he respected me and that he didn't think it was going to be an easy fight. He said he wanted to get past me and then he'd look to his future and that he hadn't underestimated me. Then they turned the mike on me and I looked on this as a golden opportunity. The press said, 'Now Jim, it's eight hours till the biggest night of your life, how do you feel?'

I overruled the question and said, 'First of all this isn't the biggest night of my life, the biggest night of my life was when I fought a better fighter than Barry McGuigan; Brian Mitchell, for the world title. I've got no respect for Barry McGuigan at all and I'm gonna go out there and smash him to pieces. I'm gonna do a job on him, I'm gonna show him no mercy and I'm gonna end his career.' And even then I was playing with his mind and I could see it in his eyes.

His parting shot to me the week before had been 'I just hope you're there' so consequently, when we climbed into the ring on the night, I waited patiently for him to arrive. When he actually got in the ring and the ref pulled us together I stuck my head in his face and said, 'I'm fucking here', and I repeated it and repeated it until I was told to shut up by the referee. But I could see that I had definitely won the mind game. And I think out of the forty reporters only one went for me, none of them had seen the inner feeling that he was living with, but I'd seen it early and played on it.

Once you'd beaten him mentally he'd got nothing left. Talking about in-fight fear Jim, how did you cope mentally when fighting someone such as Azumo Nelson, and how did you cope with in-fight fear?

Well I should imagine that everyone deals with it in a different way. My personal formula is to rehearse it, and I go through things in my mind which I think may happen. I go through all the positives and negatives, which we've already discussed and this develops the will to win the fight. I rehearse everything from in the changing room before the fight to walking down the aisle to the ring, the music in the background, the crowd cheering, everything. I rehearse what I'll do if things do go wrong, if I get knocked down I'll watch the ref as he counts, I'll get up at eight and walk behind the referee to give me a few more seconds.

So I don't really get in-fight fear too much, Geoff, because I've already dealt with every situation that can happen in the ring weeks before I even get in there. I still get nervous but I don't mind that because that tells me that I'm sharp, I'm ready.

Me and Chris Pyat, who is a good friend of mine who went on to win a world title, went to the Commonwealth Games in Brisbane in 1982. We were mates and I was the first lad from the England team to box and at that stage of the game I was, like, so psyched up to win. There were nine of us in the team and I didn't want to be the first one to go out [lose]. I was fighting a Zambian who was one of the tips to win the gold medal and I knew it was a tough draw.

I was so fired up. I was really in tremendous physical shape and I remember getting in the ring and after the first round I was exhausted, I was really tired. Anyway, I won the fight eventually on a 4–1 majority verdict and Pyat said to me after the fight 'You're too tense, Jim, you're just so fired up, you're so psyched up, you're always talking about boxing, you're always thinking about boxing. You've got to learn to switch off'. And that was when I learned what he was saying.

The next fight, which was two days later, I deliberately did it. I did exactly what Pyat told me basically. I was against another good opponent who was Ugandan, again a tough, tough fight. I got in there and I boxed superbly, didn't blow once. And from that day onwards, I think it was like an inner message on how to feel.

It's just knowing when to switch on and when to switch off so that you don't waste any energy outside of the fight.

People say to me, 'How can you switch off?' Fighters ask me, 'How can you switch it off when it's constantly there, the nagging thing that is always there?' People say, 'I've tried everything, I've gone to the pictures, I've watched films, I've done this and that but the fight is still there. You say you just switch off but how can you just switch off?' Again, it's self-control. I've got a thing, there's a time for work and there's a time for play and I've mastered it because I do literally switch off completely.

How do you deal with aftermath?

I think it becomes a way of life. I set myself to become world champion but I also say to myself, 'If it goes smoothly that's a plus, but somewhere along that road it ain't all gonna be smooth, there's gonna be bumps, you get cut eyes, you may get knocked out.' All sorts of things can happen but at the end of the day I still want to travel the journey so consequently I do all the build-up of the positive.

With the negatives, well like you say with the aftermath when the result goes the other way, like the Nelson fight, then you sort of sit yourself down and you're obviously very disappointed, but you've already dealt with the possibility of defeat beforehand. I think the only fighters that are destroyed by one defeat only get destroyed because they didn't anticipate the possibility of it happening beforehand. They've probably tried to block it out so when it has actually become a reality it knocks them for six and takes all their confidence away.

What would you advise people who are struggling with the fear syndrome Jim, not necessarily boxers but anyone in any walk of life?

In 1989 I'd lost to Brian Mitchell in a world title fight, and I felt that my career had hit a level. I felt like I needed change, like a player at a football club, I felt like I needed to move on. Barry Hearn was new on the scene in boxing. Everyone at the Royal Oak [a professional boxing stable] had been unhappy with one thing or another along the line; Frank Bruno, Mark Kaylor, Charlie Magri, David Dent, I could go through the whole stable. Everyone had spoken about it but not done it, I was actually the first one to leave the stable. They called me the Pied Piper in the end because everyone followed me. I was the one who said, 'I ain't gonna have this, I've got to move on.' I had a mortgage and all sorts of things around me that made it hard to take chances. I had to make a decision. It was November and my contract ran up to March but I walked; I went my own way because I wanted to better myself.

It was a very sad day when I walked in the gym and shook hands with Barry Mason and Frank Bruno and all the others and they all said 'respect' to me. Because they knew what I was doing, they wanted to go but none of them had stood up and done it.

It was the same thing, being positive, even though it was outside of the combat thing it was about PMA; I knew what I wanted and I just went for it. I went with Barry Hearn, who was not well known in the boxing world at that time so everything could quite easily have backfired on me. I was in a position with Terry Lawless where everything was cuddly, I was getting fair money, and although I was never happy with what I got for my world title fight, it was paying my mortgage and I was one of the boys as it were.

So you had a real comfort zone there?
Yeah, very much so, and in the end I had to go out on my own. I remember Frank Bruno saying to me 'Jimmy Mac, I take my hat off to you, I always respected what you did and I wish I had done it three or four years ago.'

I'd ask people to try and be as single-minded as me. If it doesn't work out and it was the wrong decision, at least you can look yourself in the mirror and know that you were big enough to stand up and be counted.

Thanks very much Jim.

Interview 5:
Robin Horsfall, Former SAS Soldier

Robin Edward Horsfall was one of the SAS soldiers involved in the Iranian Embassy siege in London. He has now left the forces and is currently a self-employed paramedic and karate instructor.

Robin, one of the things that I found particularly interesting about you, in respect to the fact that you have led such a colourful and varied life, was the fact that you said in your self-defence book Unleash the Lioness that probably the bravest thing you can remember doing was standing up to a bully as a fifteen-year-old boy soldier.
Yeah, I think that's true. You see I was brought up without a father really. I had a stepfather who married my mother with three kids and my most specific memories of him now, looking back, were of him kicking and beating me; those are the things that stand out most to me. I don't hold it against him now. When I joined the Army I hadn't had that masculine guidance as I had grown up. So when I joined the Army with all these lads who had come from up north and some of the other rougher parts of the country, who were fairly intelligent lads because they had been selected for the junior leaders battalion, the change of characters that I was exposed to was quite dramatic. Very different from the quiet place where I had been brought up.

I made the mistake of getting a bit physical with one of these lads then leaving and not fighting back. From that point onwards for about fifteen months everyone went for me because I was a soft target, I never really turned around and fought any of them back. I'd back off, walk away and then all the evil, dirty, young men's tricks would start; getting darts thrown in your back when you turned around, having your bed turned over in the night when you were asleep. You were a victim because you were vulnerable. All of this was a big culture shock to me; I'd lived all of my life with people that didn't do that type of thing so I'd never seen that side of human nature.

I was in an environment that I didn't understand, not knowing what to do in certain circumstances. It took me a long time to figure out. I was pushed and pushed and pushed and I got to the point where the worm either turned or stayed a victim for the rest of its life. Finally this other lad decided that he was going to have a go at me and I just snapped really, I just thought, 'Bollocks, I'm not putting up with this any more' and I went for it. Something clicked in my brain that I'd never experienced before, that kind of 'sod it, what have I got to lose?' That was at the age of fifteen and it was a big step for me because it meant, 'right, I'm prepared to fight now' and I was prepared to accept that I might get my head kicked in.

Do you think that that is why most people don't succeed in life and remain victims, because they can't force themselves to make that step?

I think that taking chances has a lot to do with knowledge, education, experience and determination, it's down to evaluating the gains and the losses. Big businessmen are not people that gamble, they are people that evaluate the odds then go with the strongest chance; they don't do foolish things.

But there is always a risk, and that is what separates dreamers from doers?
Oh yeah. In terms of not succeeding in life, I think that the people that do succeed in life are very often the most insecure people. I think that the aggression and drive that special forces' soldiers and top businessmen have comes from a desire to prove something either to themselves or to other people.

If you take the special forces, the top special forces are the SAS guys as far as I'm concerned. The SAS guys are brilliant at achieving things, they are given a task and they will achieve it, they've gone through that selection process, and you really have to put yourself on the line and beyond it to get through. To want to do that you have to have something inside you saying 'I've got to prove this' and usually when you're a lad that age you're proving it to yourself because you're very insecure. You go into battle and you're doing the most outrageous things because you want people to see that you're brave, you're super, you're wonderful. So a lot of the time it is just a desire to prove something to yourself or to others.

How do you overcome the very tangible fear of jumping out of an aeroplane?
I think the biggest thing about overcoming fear is knowledge. There's an old RAF regiment saying: 'knowledge dispels fear'. And that doesn't just apply to parachuting, it applies to everything in life. If you're stood on a nightclub door and someone comes up to you and you are immediately threatened, you immediately look at him and use your previous experience or knowledge. You think, 'How is he standing? What has he got in his hands? Is there anybody with him? Is there somebody behind me, where is my back-up?'

You take in all of that information and as you evaluate the danger, you look at his build, his stance, his hands and your back-up and you realise that the threat is diminishing very quickly so the fear starts diminishing and the control in your mind starts to increase.

When you haven't got any knowledge or previous experience, and when you haven't got any of that big word TRAINING, and you're standing there and a guy comes up acting aggressively, you don't have anything to fall back on and somebody is saying, 'Right, you're here, deal with it', what are you going to do? You could panic, you could freeze, you could overdo it and hurt someone badly because you don't have any knowledge or any training.

It's the same with parachuting; the first thing they do is show you how the parachute works, how it opens and what it's made of. They teach you all the emergencies, you go through the drills until eventually you're dangling through that door on your first parachute jump and all that information is sitting in your head. How many parachutes don't open, what happens if they don't open, there's something I can do, I can pull this reserve; all those drills that you've gone through are there. And it's training.

And that would apply to any fear, Robin?
Yes.

Regarding the Iranian Embassy siege, there must have been a tremendous amount of anticipation, how did you learn to cope with that?
Well yeah, because, if I remember rightly, the siege lasted for seven days and it went just like a training exercise, like the exercises that we'd done previously. People used to think that

there was a set counter-terrorist team in the regiment at that time – there wasn't. There were four squadrons and every squadron used to do four months and then another squadron would take over, everybody was trained in it. It was my second trip on the counter-terrorist team and we'd done these exercises where you'd go and sit in this building and you'd do 'immediate action drills'. You'd do this drill and that drill and you'd do getting through windows drills; eventually you'd do an attack and you'd do this option and that option and you attack aeroplanes and you attack buses and you attack buildings and you attack ships, you cover everything. And then eventually one day, there you are waiting to go on another exercise to Scotland and buff, the Iranian Embassy siege starts. I think it was on a Friday afternoon or a Saturday morning and that night we were in the building next door to the Iranian Embassy, the Royal College of Surgeons on Prince's Gate. It was a big day in my life, it really was.

People asked me about it afterwards and said 'it must have been terribly frightening', but it wasn't that frightening. There were fifty-four of us going into the building against eight terrorists so we knew that we were going to win. However, you don't know how many you're going to lose while you're doing that because by the time we actually did the attack we knew that they had hand grenades, we knew they had explosives and automatic weapons.

Which comes back to knowledge dispelling fear again.

Yes, that's right. We knew where they were in the building, we knew what we had, we'd practised this again and again. When it actually came down to the assault things went wrong. One of the guys was abseiling down the building and his foot went through the window so we had to initiate the 'go' before we were 100 per cent ready because we were going to blow all the windows and doors at the same time. You probably saw the guys on the balcony putting the charges on; well that was supposed to be a sneaky-peaky job and we were going to converge on the terrorists all at once, but of course when we got 'Go go go' because the guy's foot went through the window, we ran across and jumped back and 'whoom' [simulates the sound of the explosion], in we go – it was very dramatic. In you go, and it was just like a training drill.

What was your job in the Iranian Embassy siege?
My job was to stay on the back door and if there seemed to be a breakdown anywhere we (a guy called Ginge Young and me) were supposed to charge in and support the group that was in trouble. But the communications went down and the AC turned around and sent us in anyway. So we went in and at the time the hostages were just starting to come down the stairs.

There are a thousand stories that relate around this but I'm saving them for a book one day [laughs]. But lots of lovely little personal things happened, not superhero things but personal things. For instance, there was a guy called Toad, that was his nickname, and he gets up to the first floor and there's bullets coming through the door, and he had to go along the landing and through this door. And all the lads are like, 'Come on, come on!' And Toad was an old soldier with a lot of experience and he just sat down on the top of the stairs and pulled his gas mask back and said, 'I think we'd better sit here for a minute.' Then the bullets stopped coming through the door and he pulled his gas mask back over his face and said, 'OK, let's do it.'

The whole job took seven minutes. I went in at the bottom, the hostages were coming down the stairs and there was a voice at the top of the stairs shouting 'He's a terrorist,' and we see this guy coming down. There's a guy called Rusty, a guy called Gerry and me at the bottom of the stairs and we see the terrorist coming down the stairs and he's got a hand grenade. Nobody can open fire because there are hostages in the field of view, which is all training, everybody knew that they couldn't open fire. Now as he came clear at the bottom of the stairs the three of us let go [shot him]. As he dropped, the hand grenade just rolled along the floor.

We then cleared the building but there were mistakes made. There was a guy stuck on a rope who got burned because he messed up his abseiling; the building caught fire; there was one of the officers who was inside the building panicking because of the fire. It was my job to stand there and make sure that everyone in front of me was out before I started to move, but he had lost it, so I got hold of him and said, 'Listen, get fucking out!' and I threw him towards the door and he went out.

I made sure that everyone else was out and then it was my turn. There were two or three people [SAS officers] in the building who acted poorly under pressure. There were two guys down in the cellar who were experienced old soldiers who emptied three magazines of ammunition into nothing, because they were panicking and these were the old and bold. These were the guys that you looked up to and thought, 'Oh, they've done it all before.'

So everyone can make mistakes?
Well it wasn't a mistake, they just didn't have the training, they thought that they knew it all. They'd got to the point in life where they thought they didn't need to learn anything else, and that's a very dangerous stage to get to where you think that you're the bees knees and you can no longer learn anything.

So you can never really afford to become complacent.
That's right.

Do you think that applies to most things in life?
I think it applies to everything in life.

Do the SAS do anything specifically on fear management?
No, not exactly, but a lot of your training is absolutely outrageous.

Could you relate any of the things to us?
Oh yeah, sure. When you're in the regiment you are either in mountain troop, air troop, mobility troop or boat troop. Now everybody is a paratrooper, but free-fallers are jumping [parachuting] at 25,000 feet at night with spiralling bundles in the middle and you're trying to fly around them. You know with pitch blackness and oxygen it was all pretty hairy stuff from 25,000 feet. I was with the mountain troop and it's amazing how many guys will do free-fall but won't go up a rock face.

Mountain climbing itself, especially when you're leading, is a unique experience because it's you against the rock and if you make a mistake, if you go the wrong way or you get stuck, then you'd better have some protection, your skill had better be adequate otherwise you're going to fall and you're going to die. So you're confronted with fear in a sense where you've got to be analytical and you've got to realise that you must work out what comes next.

Like in my book [*Unleash the Lioness*] I talk about being stuck on a rock face one day when I didn't have enough protection. I knew I was on the right route but I couldn't find the next hole and I got into a situation which you should never get into when you're rock climbing: where you can't step back down to the last hole. I was stuck in a position where my wrists were getting cramped, my feet were getting cramped and I was going to fall and I knew it was a long way down. My number two was around the corner, he couldn't see me so even if he tightened the rope I didn't have enough protection to stop me from hitting the rock below.

I had a choice: to lunge up and hope to find it [a good grip hole] or stand still and eventually fall and hope that my fairy godmother came along. So I lunged and whacked straight into this hole. I made a decision based on the worst-case scenario of doing nothing, and this is the worst-case scenario of doing something, but actually making yourself do something when at that point you may get it wrong and die is very hard, but I went and there it was. But if I hadn't jumped I'd have died anyway, and I knew that, so I made the decision and that decision saved my life.

So what they did was to put you into situations that were as fearful as the combat situations that you were likely to be exposed to?

Yes, actually I often found the simulated situations more frightening than the real ones. But yes, when we went into a live situation it felt just like a training drill.

When you did stints like Northern Ireland how did you cope with that constant anticipation of conflict?
With long drawn out periods like that you've got a time frame that you're working on and you just have to accept. I think that's the big word: acceptance. You have to accept the worst-case scenario. OK, I could die. Once you've accepted it you can deal with it. That doesn't mean that you're not frightened, but it certainly does take the bite away and then you can work at it 100 per cent because you've already told yourself that you're prepared to accept the worst-case scenario.

Do you think that this is the universal way of getting a grip on fear, by accepting in your mind the worst thing that can happen?
I remember reading once that great Samurai would accept death every morning. He would tell himself that today he would die in battle, then he'd accept that he was going to die so he could operate without fear at 100 per cent efficiency. If he came out of the battle at the end of the day still alive and with everything intact it was a bonus. It's extreme but it's the same thing and it does work. I also remember a great statement from the book *Dune* that I think is very apt and it is 'fear is the mind killer'. It's true, it really is true.

Yes, that's brilliant, I'd agree with that.
I think that the crucial things needed to deal with fear are information and training. If you have the information, the knowledge, fear is often completely dispelled and if it isn't you can deal with it through training.

Finally, Robin, what advice would you offer people who may be struggling with the fear syndrome, not necessarily in a combat sense but any kind of adversity?
Whatever it is you're frightened of, train yourself or get training to deal with it, to understand it. To be able to overcome a fear you've got to understand that fear, the more you understand about the thing that is threatening you, the less of a threat it becomes and the less dangerous it becomes. Eventually, the more you understand it, it almost goes away and very often you realise that there was no real danger there in the first place and that it wasn't anything to worry about.

If you want to do a bungee jump, go and study bungee jumping, understand what the rope is made of, understand how high the crane goes, understand the pressures and the pounds per square inch and everything that goes into it, then you can go and do it because all of a sudden it is no longer that scary. First study whatever it is that you fear and then confront it. You may no longer have to confront whatever it was because the fear may be completely dispelled. So you no longer have to prove anything because you are not scared of it any more.

Robin, thanks very much for your time.

Epilogue

As I have said throughout the book, admit your fears, learn to understand them and then systematically confront them one by one until they have all been dispelled. Expect adversity; that is the price you may have to pay for a braver life, but it will be worth it. I wish you, whoever you may be, the very best of luck with your endeavours.

J.T.B.

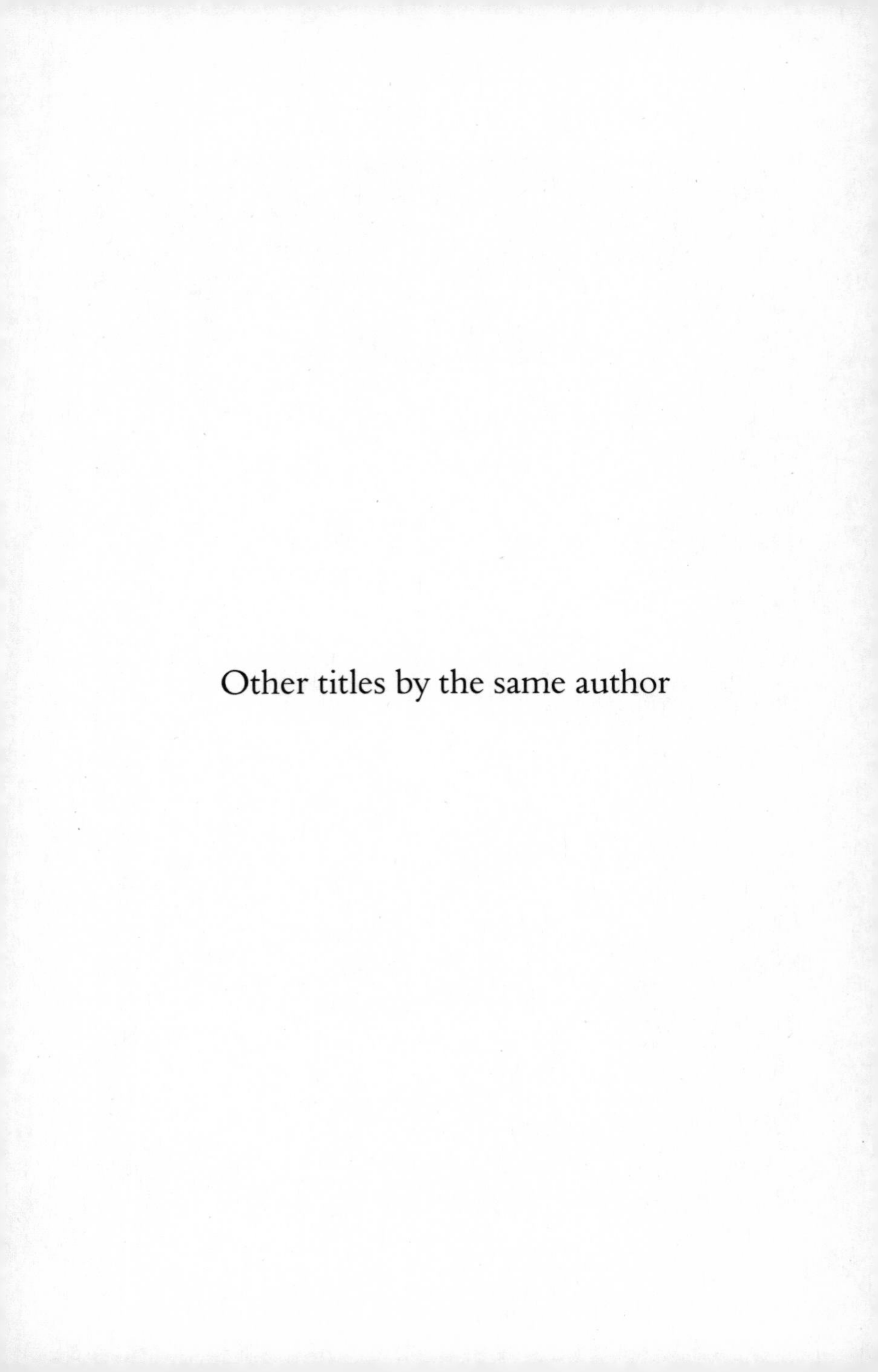

Other titles by the same author

geoff thompson

the elephant and the twig

the art of positive thinking

14 golden rules for success and happiness

The Elephant and the Twig

The Art of Positive Thinking

Geoff Thompson

£7.99 Pb

ISBN: 1 84024 264 7
ISBN 13: 978 1 84024 264 5

In India, young elephants are trained in obedience by being tied to an immovable object like a tree. No matter how hard the baby elephant pulls it cannot break free, and eventually, after trying to break away and being thwarted time and again, it believes that it cannot escape, no matter what it does. Ultimately, a fully-grown adult weighing several tons can be tied to a twig and won't even try to escape.

Do you ever feel that you are tied to an immovable object and can't break free? That you couldn't possibly give that presentation, that you would never be able to go it alone in business, or that you have to remain stuck in a social and lifestyle rut as there is no other alternative? This book argues that what ties you down and prevents you from realising your potential is only a 'twig'. Geoff guides you through the process of breaking the negative thinking that binds us and reveals the '14 Golden Rules for Success and Happiness'.

'One of the best new writers ever to come out of Britain'

Ray Winstone

geoff thompson

shape shifter

transform your life in 1 day

powerful advice on personal development

Shape Shifter
Transform Your Life in One Day
Powerful Advice on Personal Development

Geoff Thompson

£7.99 Pb

ISBN: 1 84024 444 5

ISBN 13: 978 1 84024 444 1

Do you believe that the world's leading lights are gifted from birth or even just plain lucky? In this groundbreaking guide, **Geoff Thompson** demonstrates that *anyone* with average ability and a strong desire to succeed can do so in any chosen field.

The former bouncer and factory floor sweeper, now a BAFTA award-winning film-maker, author of 30 books, acclaimed screenwriter and martial arts expert, knows this better than most. From Day One, this book will provide inspiration and prove that everyone has the potential to achieve their own personal ambition.

In *Shape Shifter*, the first self-help guide of its kind, you will learn:

- that shape shifting is our birthright as a creative species;
- how to practise the art of personal transformation, step by step;
- that with the right strategy and approach, success is always a choice.

'...highly readable and engaging...genuinely inspiring... refreshingly down to earth, peppered with humour and humility'

The Big Issue

geoff thompson

stress buster

how to stop stress from killing you

Stress Buster

How to Stop Stress Killing You

Geoff Thompson

£7.99 Pb

ISBN: 1 84024 509 3
ISBN 13: 978 1 84024 509 7

In our increasingly hectic society we are under constant pressure to get the best results, the top job, a better car or a bigger house. For many reasons, stress can become a major problem affecting our relationships and even our health. Stress can ruin lives, and most people don't know how to cope with it – or how they can use it as an energy force.

If you're always getting angry in the car, at home or at work, if you constantly feel out of balance, then this book is for you. It will help you identify the causes of stress in your life, and shows you how to deal with them in a practical way. With true-life examples, clear explanations and relevant advice, it's an indispensable aid to overcoming stress.

'A superb book... a very good common sense look at stress... the secret ways to harness the beast called stress are shared with the reader in an easy to read and understanding way. This book will seriously transform your life!'

Scottish Health News

'A wide-ranging book and a reassuring read for anyone feeling stressed. Guaranteed to make you take a fresh look at your approach to life'

M2 Best Books

www.geoffthompson.com